Woodworking Together

Projects for kids and their families

Woodworking Together

Projects for kids and their families

Alan & Gill
Bridgewater

TAB **TAB BOOKS**

Blue Ridge Summit, PA

FIRST EDITION
FIRST PRINTING

© 1993 by **TAB Books.**
TAB Books is a division of McGraw-Hill, Inc.

Library of Congress Cataloging-in-Publication Data

Bridgewater, Alan.
  Woodworking together : projects for kids and their families / by
Alan and Gill Bridgewater.
    p. cm.
  Includes index.
  ISBN 0-8306-2164-4 (pbk.)
  1. Woodwork. I. Bridgewater, Gill. II. Title.
TT185.B74 1992
684'.08—dc20   92-24859
                                               CIP

TAB Books offers software for sale. For information and a catalog, please contact
TAB Software Department, Blue Ridge Summit, PA 17294-0850.

Acquisitions Editor: Stacy Varavvas-Pomeroy
Book Editor: April D. Nolan
Director of Production: Katherine G. Brown
Book Design: Jaclyn J. Boone
Cover Design: Graphics Plus, Hanover, PA.
Cover Photograph: Thompson Photography, Baltimore, MD.   BH20

Contents

Acknowledgments

We would like to thank all those people who helped us with this book.
A special thanks must go to:

Julian and Glyn Bridgewater—two wonderful sons to be proud of. This book draws its inspiration from all their hammer-and-nail activities when they were kids! Remember the cross-bow? the tree house? and all Glyn's boxes??

Glen Tizard for supplying the Draper fretsaw and Roger Buse for supplying the Hegner scroll saw.

Steven Morran of Loctite for supplying the Super Glue 3. It's amazing!

Humbrol Faints for supplying the paints.

Introduction

Children grow up so quickly! One moment they are in diapers, and then—before you can say, "Please, no more PTA meetings!"—they have grown up and left the nest.

It's important that you find ways of making your time with your children count. Woodworking together—parents and kids working side by side to create all kinds of woodworking projects—is a uniquely wonderful way for parents and children to get to know each other.

I can clearly remember when I was a kid—I must have been about 8 years old—being shown by my grandfather how to set out a piece of wood with a try square and pencil, and how to saw the wood to size. I remember long summer days spent with wood, saws, and nails. We measured, and we cut, and we hammered, and we had a rare old time. And then at long last, after much sweating and getting covered in dust and wood shavings, we settled down in the garden with our tea and cake, and sat back and admired our woodworking efforts. It was a wonderful experience that I shall never ever forget. Okay, so in all truth, our lean-to porch was not a pretty sight—lots of splinters, wibbley-wobbley edges, dribbles of glue, and mistakes—but when I look back at those summer days of long ago, what I remember most of all are the feelings of pride and accomplishment when my grandfather solemnly declared that, all things considered, it was a job well done. Those were happy days.

And so as the wheel turned, I married, we worked alongside our own children, and now our sons are almost grown up and—who knows? Maybe in a few years time we will be showing our grandchildren how to hold a saw and bang in a nail.

Woodworking Together is about all the many and various joyful hands-on pleasures of adults and children working together on woodworking projects. Sawing wood, hammering nails, spreading glue, cutting joints, sanding, painting, and varnishing are all exciting. But don't think that the pleasure is only in the making—not a bit of it. You and the kids will find that the projects are exciting and stimulating in their own right. A wooden airplane, a console shelf, a sled, a pair of stilts—they are all great fun! By working through the projects in turn, you and the kids will not only cover all the primary hand-tool woodworking techniques, but along the way you will create a good number of useful objects.

Each project has been carefully considered and designed so that there is an easy flow and link-up between age, skill level, and the items being made. In addition, there is an age-interest-skill progression from toys and games, through to small items of bedroom furniture, sports items, study equipment, and jewelry. For example, with the first project, making a bathtub yacht, not only is the Kids'-eye view introduction aimed at 7- to 8-year-olds, but the yacht, the tools, the techniques, and all the making and doing stages are aimed specifically at children of that age. Our thinking is that not only will the average 7- to 8-year-old be motivated to make the yachts, but because skill level and tool manipulation have been very carefully considered, you will (with our guidance) easily be able to show them the way.

The same goes for all the other projects in the book. They have all been shaped to suit the interests and likely skill level of specific age ranges. And, of course, towards the end of the book, when the projects are aimed at older children—14- to 15-year-olds—so the guidance and skill levels change accordingly. There are projects for kiddies and parents working together, there are projects for teenagers, there are projects for older children to make for kid brothers and sisters, and so on.

Now you might or might not be an experienced woodworker—no matter! With our Beginner's Guide (beginning on page xiii), and caregiver's guide sections (in each chapter), we will put you on the right road. We warn you of possible problems, we describe how junior or missy might have difficulties with such-and-such a tool, we describe the joints, we describe the fixings, we illustrate the working stages, and so on. We appreciate that you—a mom, dad, granny or grandpa—might not know the difference between a coping saw, a clamp and a cucumber, so we iron out the wrinkles and guide you through. The projects are illustrated, there are working drawings and design templates, tools and materials lists, painting grids, step-by-step illustrations, special tips, and problem solving sections. But be warned: By the time you have worked through the projects, your home will be much beautified with woodwork, your workshop will be full of off-cuts, and you and the kids will be flat out and exhausted. As a family you will have had a marvelously enriched time. Keep in mind that—yes!—*Woodworking Together* is about creating craft items in wood, but more than that, it is about having fun, and about the pure joy and pleasure of working together. Mothers and sons, fathers and daughters, all working towards a common aim. Touching and helping hands, laughing at mistakes, and working together to create items in wood are all exciting quality-time experiences that should not be missed!

What else to say, except that *Woodworking Together* is about physical well-being, personal involvement, and the joys of working and playing together as a family. Best of luck!

Beginner's guide

How many tools does a woodworking family need? Should we tell you in detail how best to use pencils, rulers, saws, chisels, and drills? Should we take it that you are more than just a beginner? It's all a bit of a problem! Well, we have carried out our own *Woodworking Together* survey—that is, we have talked it over with our two sons, we have asked all the kids in the neighborhood, we have talked it over with the man in the wood yard, we have discussed it at length with the editor of our woodworking magazine—and, of course, we have our teaching, writing, and woodworking know-how to call upon. The good news is that all parties are in complete agreement that woodworking families—moms, dads, grannies, grandpas, aunts, uncles, and all the kids—need as much help and advice as possible. Okay, so maybe minute details on everything from saws, sandpaper, and setting out are a bit of a drag, but in the context of children working in a potentially dangerous environment, such information is absolutely necessary.

How to use a tenon saw, how to use a bench hook, how to apply the paint, the smell of the wood, the crisp, butter-colored shavings as they curl up from the plane—mmm, beautiful!

Calipers, coping saws, close grain, crosscut saws, chisels, and clamps . . . these are all part and parcel of the wonderful quality-time adventure that is *Woodworking Together*!

TOOLS, TERMS, TIPS, AND TECHNIQUES

acrylic paint An easy-to-use, water-based, quick-drying, PVA-type paint. Acrylics are the perfect paint for kids and for woodwork. Acrylic can be used straight from the can or tube, the colors are bright, they are fast drying, and the brushes can easily be washed in cold water. Once in place, acrylics are hard-wearing and completely nontoxic. That said, as most woodwork gets a lot of handling, it's a good idea to protect the painted surfaces with a couple of coats of clear, high-shine varnish.

beech A heavy pleasant-to-work, yellow-orange, hardwood, perfect for general woodwork. Beech works well and takes a good finish. It is very useful for making complex profiles and hard-edged details. If you are looking to make toys or around-the-house bits and pieces, then you can't do better than use beech.

bench hook A very useful easy-to-make sawing aid, in use, it is hooked over the edge of the bench or secured in the vice, the workpiece is butted hard up-against the hook and held with one hand, while the saw is operated with the other hand (FIG. G-1).

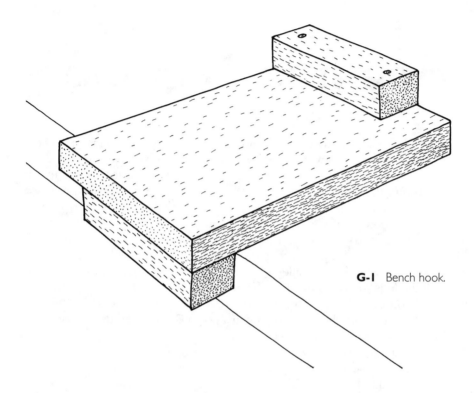

G-1 Bench hook.

blank Any block, slab, disc, or length of prepared ready-to-work wood might be termed a *blank*.

bradawl A small handle-and-spike tool used for making starter holes for screws, nails, and drills.

broomstick dowel A round section wooden dowel or rod. See *dowel*.

brushes We use flat brushes for varnishing, long-haired, fine-point brushes for details, broad brushes for large areas of flat paint, and so on. When it's time to paint small decorative details, we favor the soft-haired sable and nylon brushes used by watercolor artists. Encourage the kids to wash the brushes as soon as they are done with them, and then dry them well and store them with the heads tight-bound with plastic film. A well-kept brush will improve with use.

butt joint Butt joints are used where two pieces of wood need to be joined flush. Mating faces are glued, butted together face-to-face, and then fixed with pins or screws. For greater strength butt joints can be reinforced with inside-corner blocks, and/or metal angle plates/brackets (FIG. G-2).

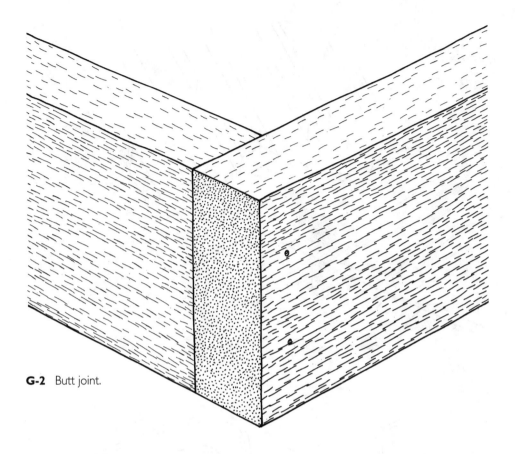

G-2 Butt joint.

calipers A two-legged measuring instrument used for checking widths and diameters. In the context of kids and woodwork, it's best to use a pair that has a positive screw adjustment.

carton card Salvaged cardboard packaging is very useful for making patterns, working models and templates. If you or the kids can't figure out from the drawings how such-and-such a woodworking detail is going to look when it has been built, then it's a good idea to make a swift mock-up with card, sticky tape and paper clips.

centerlines One or more lines that mark out the center of a symmetrical form or image. In the context of basic woodwork—a box or board—there are usually two centerlines: one that runs across the width and one that runs along the length.

chisels We favor bevel-edge chisels. We generally use four widths: ¼ inch, ½ inch, ¾ inch and 1 inch. It's best to use a chisel width that is slightly narrower than the groove/channel being cut (FIG. G-3).

clamps, cramps, and holdfasts Devices used for holding the workpiece secure while it is being worked. There are G-clamps, C-clamps, strap clamps, hold-

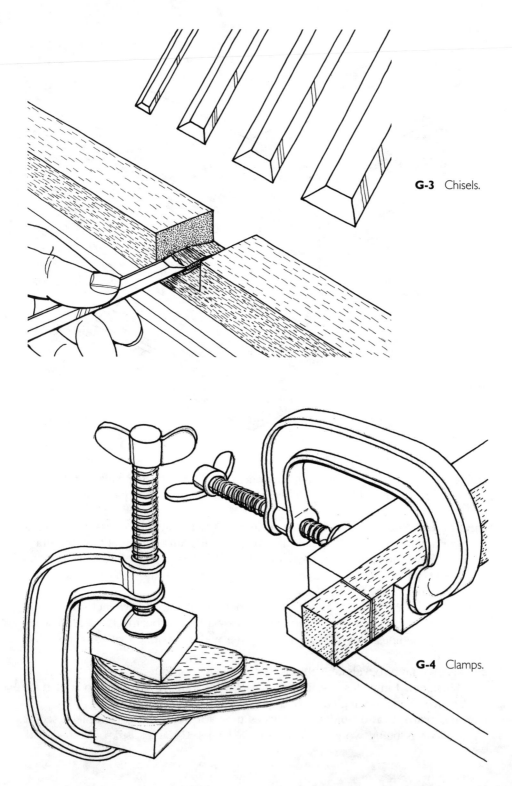

G-3 Chisels.

G-4 Clamps.

downs, holdfasts, and so on. In use, it is best to protect the workpiece by setting an off-cut waster set between it and the jaws/head of the holdfast/clamp. If your tool kit doesn't run to more than a couple of clamps, you can always make do with a rope and twist-stick garotte type clamp, or you can even strap the project up with sticky tape (FIG. G-4).

Be warned: When the workpiece is being drilled, cut with a chisel, or otherwise worked, it must be held firm and secure: You do need a bench vice.

close-grained wood A term used to describe wood that has regularly spaced annual rings. In the context of small items of woodwork, always make sure that your chosen wood is splinter proof and generally user-friendly. Although we favor working with easy-to-use pale colored hardwoods such as lime/linden, sycamore, beech, and jelutong, there are, of course, many other equally suitable types. If in doubt, have a word with a specialist supplier.

compasses A two-legged hand-held instrument used for drawing circles and arcs. We use a long-legged, multipurpose, screw-operated type with a pen-holding attachment and an extension arm. See *dividers*.

coping saw A small, flexible bladed frame saw used for cutting curves, holes and profiles in thin section wood. A good saw for kids, coping saws are relatively inexpensive so you could consider setting each child up with his or her own saw. Of course beginners tend to break a lot of blades, but then again, the blades are inexpensive and easy to fit. A really good all-round saw for a woodworking family (FIG. G-5).

countersink To make a cone-shaped depression in a drilled hole so that the head of a bolt or screw can be sunk below the surface. A countersink can be made with a small, hand-held, twist-and-turn tool, or with a countersink drill bit.

craft knife A knife with a short, sharp, strong, easy-to-change blade. We tend to use two such knives, a fine-point scalpel for designing and model making, and a Stanley-type knife for general cutting, trimming, and scoring.

crosscut saw A general-purpose saw—usually about 24–26 inches long, with 8–9 points to the inch. Good for cutting across the grain and for cutting large sheets of plywood down to size. A relatively easy-to-use saw.

cutouts The shapes that make up the project; the sawn profiles as they come off the saw. Although just about any component might be termed a cutout, we tend to use the term in the context of thin wood, especially plywood. See also *profile*.

designing The process of working out all the shapes, structures, forms, functions, and details. The following steps are used.

1. Draw inspiration from traditional originals, past projects, items glimpsed in museums, and old books.

2. Modify the size, shape, and imagery to suit our own needs.

3. Make working models from bits of wood, card, string, and modeling clay.

4. Make further modifications and adjustments to suit our tools and materials.

5. Finally, draw up full size measured designs.

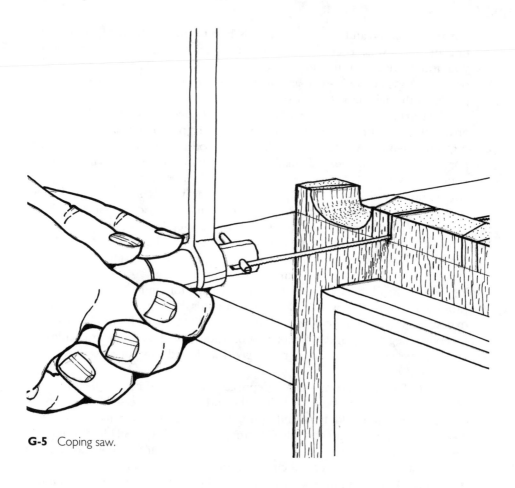

G-5 Coping saw.

dividers A two-legged compass-like instrument used for stepping off measurements and scribing circles. Simply fix the required radius by adjusting the screw-thread wheel (FIG. G-6).

double-sided sticky tape A tape that is sticky on both sides; good for holding pieces of plywood together while cutting out identical multiple shapes.

dowel Ready-to-use, round section wood is one of the woodworker's primary materials. Dowel is sold in diameters that range from ⅛ inch, ¼ inch, ⅜ inch, through to 1 inch. Dowel can be used as joint fixings, as pivots, used in the context of toys for axles, and so on. Preschool kiddies enjoy playing and experimenting with holes drilled in scrap wood and dowel off-cuts.

drilling holes The act of boring, sinking, or running holes through the workpiece. Depending upon the job in hand, we variously use a hand-held electric drill, a bench or press drill, a small wind-and-turn hand drill, and a brace. In the context of kids and woodwork, it's best to use a hand-operated wheelbrace drill for holes up to ¼-inch diameter, and a brace for holes from ¼ inch through to 1½ inches.

Hand drills are silent-running, inexpensive, and controllable. In use, the workpiece is backed with a scrap of wood and secured with a clamp, the angle

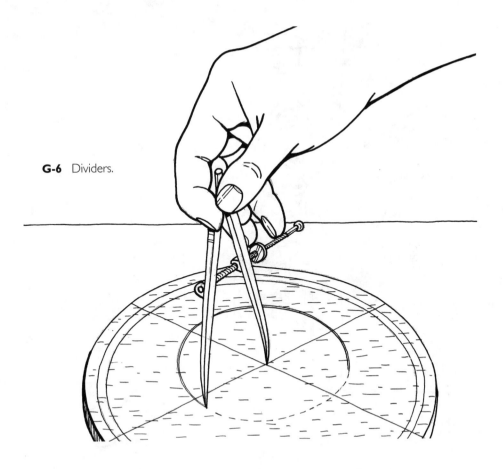

G-6 Dividers.

of the drill is checked by eye or with a try or set square, and the drill is held and steadied with one hand and set in motion with the other. Hand drills are relatively safe (FIGS. G-7 and G-8).

dust-free Wood dust can irritate the skin and generally do damage to the eyes, ears, nose and throat. This being so, try to keep the workshop dust-free, and try to avoid using exotic, possibly toxic wood types. Sweep up daily, vacuum the worksurfaces after drilling and sawing, and be aware of the problem. Some woodworkers prefer to wear a mask while they are working.

Prior to painting or varnishing, make sure that the workpiece is completely free from wood dust. Sweep up the debris, vacuum the surfaces, and then wipe the workpiece over with a dampened cloth. Ideally, painting is best done in a special dust-free area that has been set aside for that purpose.

files and rasps Files and rasps come in many shapes and sizes—everything from fine needle and riffler files, through to large two-handed rasps. We tend to use open-toothed surform rasps for large jobs, and sandpaper wrapped around sticks for small details. If the kids are using a traditional file, make sure that they

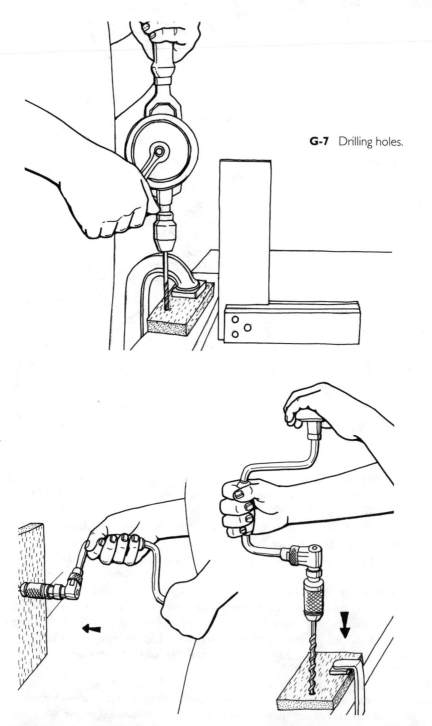

G-7 Drilling holes.

G-8 For holes larger than ¼-inch diameter, you need a brace drill, commonly called a brace-and-bit. Such a drill is for holes from ⅜ inch through to about 1½ inches diameter.

hold it in both hands, and see to it that the spiked tang is a good, secure fit in the handle.

filler A soft putty-like material used to fill splits, scratches, and cavities. We prefer to use a stable two-tube plastic/resin filler, one that can be sanded, sawn, and drilled. For small cavities, you can make a filler with sawdust and PVA adhesive.

finishing The process of filling, rubbing down, staining, painting, varnishing, waxing, and generally bringing the work to a satisfactory conclusion.

Forstner drill bit A drill bit used for boring out flat-bottomed holes. Although Forstner bits are more expensive than regular spade/flat type drill bits, they can be relied upon to produce accurate, perfect-every-time, holes.

Be warned: Some bits are designed to be used with a power drill, others with a brace, and so on. If in doubt, ask a specialist supplier.

friction fit (or push-fit) Components that can be pushed together to fit perfectly one within another. A tenon might be a good friction fit in a mortise, or a dowel might be a perfect fit in a wheel-hole. If the fit is so tight that a component needs to be hammered into place, or is so loose that it falls out, then it cannot be described as a push-fit.

gents saw A small, tenon-type brass-backed saw—really good for kids. This saw usually has a turned handle, a blade about 10 inches long, and about 20 fine-point teeth to the inch. Good for cutting fine joints, cutting thin sections of plywood and so on (FIG. G-9).

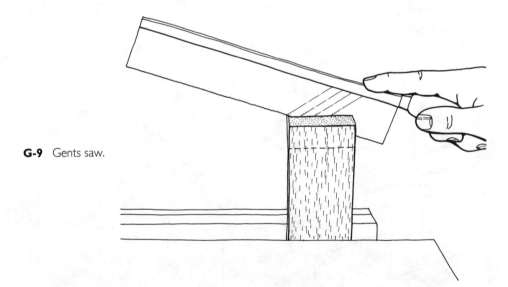

G-9 Gents saw.

glues and adhesives We currently use PVA (polyvinyl acetate) for large joints, dowel fixings, mating flat surfaces, and such like, and we use Loctite Super Glue 3 where we need to make a small, fast, very strong, dab-and-hold joint. If the kids are anxious to see how their woodworking efforts perform—small toys and such—and are raring to go, then Super Glue 3 is the answer.

gridded working drawing A drawing that has been drawn onto a scaled grid. If for example, the scale of the grid is described as being "1 grid square to 1 inch," it simply means that each one of the grid squares can be read off and transferred as being a 1-inch unit of measurement. If you want to change the scale, all you do is draw up a larger grid, and transfer the image one square at a time.

   Note: You can speed up the process by using a photocopy machine. Simply enlarge the grid squares up to the scale size.

hardware Meaning all the nails, screws, washers, nuts, bolts and hinges that you might need for a project. We use a lot of panel pins, brass screws, and nuts and bolts. For safety's sake, kiddies' playthings are best screwed, or at the very least glued and pin-fixed.

hammer We favor the use of a small lightweight hammer—called variously a pin, peen, or cross-peen hammer. If you reckon to make large items with lots of nailed joints, then you might need a large claw hammer (the claw is used for pulling out nails).

housing In the context of this book, the term *housing* is taken to mean the female half of the joint—the groove, slot, channel, notch, or hole—into which the male half of the joint is pushed, slotted or dropped.

lap joint A method of joining two pieces of wood. A full-lap joint is where a full slot is cut in one piece that is the width and thickness of the other piece. A *half-lap* or *halving* is where with two rails of equal thickness, half the thickness of each rail is cut away so that the two pieces of wood slot together for a flush fit (FIG. G-10).

   Note: From woodworker to woodworker, identical joints are given slightly different names. So for example—a "cross-halving," "crossed-half-cut-through," "crossed lap" and "crossed half-lap" are all one and the same joint.

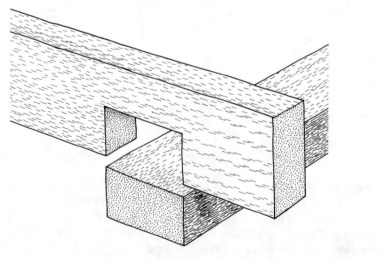

G-10 Lap joint.

maquette—see *prototype*

marking gauge A small, inexpensive tool used for marking straight, uniform lines parallel to sides and edges—really useful for setting out joints (FIG. G-11).

masking tape We use masking tape—a sticky, low-tack adhesive, paper tape—for holding down working drawings, for strapping up work that has been glued, and so on. It's a really useful, child-friendly product.

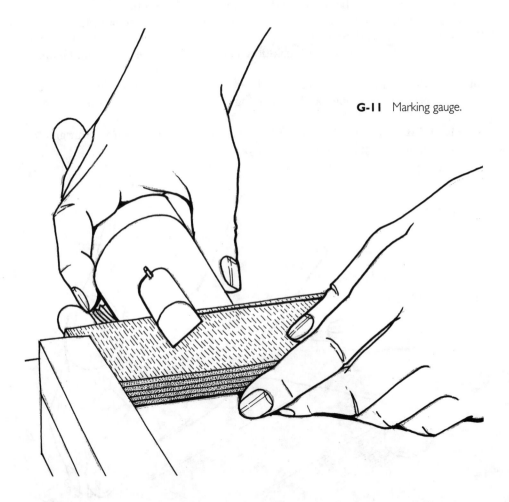

G-11 Marking gauge.

mating faces Touching parts, the faces within a joint, two pieces of wood that butt together, two faces that are to be glued together, and so on might all be described as mating faces.

modifying The process of redesigning some part of the project to suit your own needs/likes. For example, if you like such-and-such a detail but want to make it bigger, or smaller, or have it painted, or make it from a different material, or whatever, the redesigning process is generally termed *modifying*.

multicore, plywood, and multi-ply In the context of working with kids, we always use best quality, birch/white faced, multicore or multi-veneer type of plywood. Such a plywood is commonly sold in thicknesses ranging from ⅛ inch through to 1 inch. It's more economical to purchase a whole 48-x-96-inch sheet, rather than small pieces. If you can only afford a single sheet, buy the ¼-inch-thick ply, and then sandwich layers to make ½ inch, ¾ inch, or whatever. Best-quality multicore plywood can easily be cut on a scroll/fret/piercing saw, with all faces and edges being worked to a smooth and even finish.

Be warned: If you settle for using cheap-grade coarse-center plywood, then on your own head be it! The kids will find it very difficult to work, and as likely as not, the laminations will break down and the cut edges will need filling.

off-cuts Bits and pieces of scrap wood left over from other projects can be saved and used for small jobs and for making prototypes. Many wood suppliers sell very useful off-cuts.

overlap joint The simplest form of joint. Mating faces are smeared with glue and then the joint is fixed with pins (FIG. G-12).

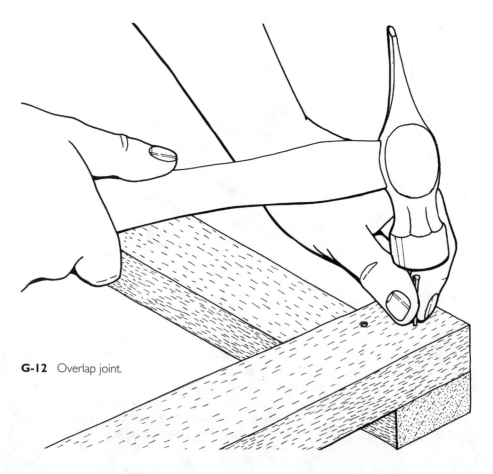

G-12 Overlap joint.

painting Ideally the painting is best done in an area that has been set apart for that purpose. We use acrylics, rather than model-maker's enamel/oil paints, because acrylics are user-friendly and nontoxic. Acrylics dry very quickly, several coats of paint can be applied in a short time, the brushes can be washed in water, and the colors are bright. *Note:* If the kids get paint on their clothes, no problem—as long as the paint is washed out under running water before it has a chance to dry. The order of work for painting is:

1. Start by making sure that the object to be painted is smooth, clean, dry, and free from dust.
2. Spend time carefully setting out all your paints and materials.
3. Consider how the object/components are going to be supported when they have been painted. You will need a line, a wire rack, or whatever.
4. Lay on a couple of base coats of matte acrylic paint.
5. Decorate with the fine-point details.
6. Finally, when the acrylic is completely dry (and not forgetting to rub down between coats), lay on a couple of coats of clear high-shine varnish.

paring The act of holding the chisel bevel-up—one hand holding and pushing on the handle, and the other holding and guiding the blade—while carefully slicing the waste back to the drawn line.

    Be warned: For safety's sake, the workpiece must always be held secure in a vice or with a clamp, and the blade must always be moving away from the body (FIG. G-13).

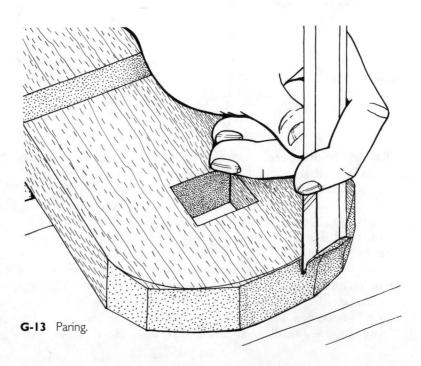

G-13 Paring.

pencils and pencil-press transferring We use a soft 2B for designing and tracing, and a hard H for pencil-press transferring, The order of work is:

1. Draw out the full-size master design.
2. Make a careful tracing.
3. Pencil in the lines at the back of the tracing with a 2B pencil.
4. Turn the tracing right-side-up and fix it to working face of the wood with tabs of sticky tape.
5. Finally, rework the traced lines with a hard pencil (FIG. G-14).

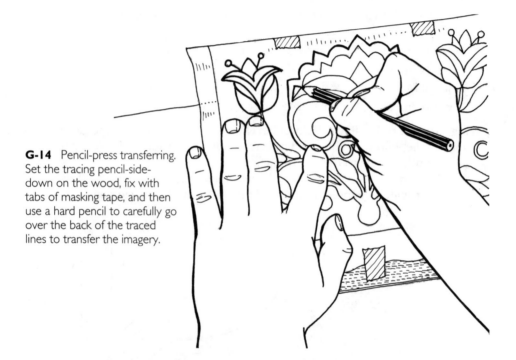

G-14 Pencil-press transferring. Set the tracing pencil-side-down on the wood, fix with tabs of masking tape, and then use a hard pencil to carefully go over the back of the traced lines to transfer the imagery.

pillar drill or drill press A large, bench-mounted electric drill with a bit-gripping chuck, and an adjustable height/angle worktable. If you plan to do a lot of woodwork, then a pillar drill is a very useful piece of machinery.

Be warned: If you have such a drill, make sure that you use the safety guard, make sure the workpiece is held secure in a vice or clamp, and never let a child use it unattended.

pilot hole A small drilled guide hole through which the blade of the scroll/fret saw can be passed, or a hole used to ensure an easy passage for a screw.

pivot In the context of this book, a pivot is the rod, bolt, shaft, or dowel on which another part might swing, turn, roll, or otherwise move.

plane A hand-held tool used for smoothing and leveling wood. We currently use two planes: a small metal bench plane and a block plane.

pliers or grips   Pliers and grips come in many shapes and sizes. We use long-nosed pliers and locking grips. Good for bending wire and such.

profiles   Although just about any cutout, silhouette, cross-section, drawn shape, or flat-fretted form, might be termed a *profile*, we tend to use the term in the context of a side view or image that is fretted from plywood.

prototype   A working model made prior to making the actual project. If you aren't quite sure how such-and-such a detail is going to work out, or if you want to make a few modifications, then you need to iron out possible problems by making a mock- up, working model, maquette, or prototype.

resin glue   A two-tube resin-to-hardener adhesive. *Be warned:* Some resin glues are tricky to use, so always read instructions.

rubbing down   The process of using sandpaper to rub the sawn profiles and sections down to a smooth, ready-to-paint finish. Working well away from the painting area, the order of work is:

1. Trim off the corners, edges, and burrs with a plane or chisel.

2. Swiftly rub over with a medium-grit sandpaper.

3. Fill cracks or holes with two-tube resin filler.

4. Finally, work through the pack of coarse-to-smooth graded sandpapers until the workpiece is smooth to the touch.

   Be warned: If you are worried about breathing in potentially harmful dust, wear a mask.

sanding and sandpaper   We purchase sandpaper (glass paper, garnet paper) in graded packs, with the grades running in degrees of coarseness or "grits," from rough to smooth. Small, difficult-to-get-at areas are best worked with the sandpaper being supported on a stick tool. When you are sanding or rubbing down a large flat surface, wrap the sandpaper around a wood or cork block, and always work in the direction of the grain. It's vital that both the wood and sandpaper are crisp and dry.

screws and screwdrivers   In the context of kids' woodwork, screws are safer and more permanent than nails. If you have a choice, use brass, chrome, or stainless steel screws with round or countersunk heads. When you are finishing, make sure that the screws are smooth to the touch and free from sharp edges and burrs. Use the correct size screwdrivers to avoid doing damage to the workpiece and the screw.

scroll saw   A fine-bladed, electric bench saw, sometimes called a jig or fretsaw, used for cutting out profiles in thin sheet wood. In use, the workpiece is pushed across the worktable and fed into the blade. The blades come in many grades, and are cheap and easy to replace. The scroll saw is safe to use, as long as you hold the whole piece fast-down on the table, work at a steady pace, and are always ready to present the blade with the line of next cut. The up-and-down jigging action of the blade results in a swift, fine, good-every-time cut.

We currently use two fretsaws—a Draper and a Hegner. They can cut anything from thin veneers through to 2-inch-thick wood. They have tilt blades, they are safe and easy to use, and they have rapid blade change. All in all, they are the perfect machines for a woodworking family (FIG. G-15).

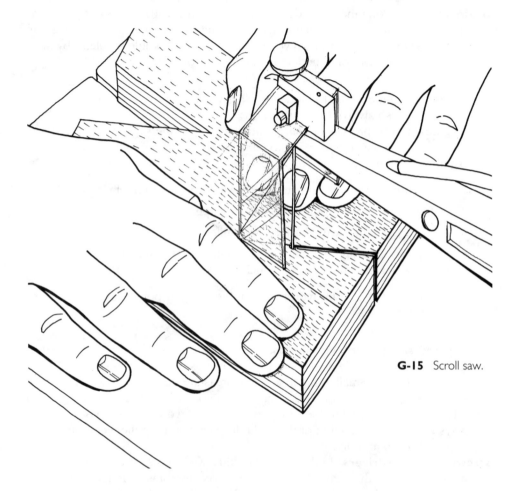

G-15 Scroll saw.

The order of work for cutting out an enclosed hole or window is:

1. Release the blade tension and unhitch the blade.
2. Slide the workpiece on the cutting table and pass the blade through the pilot hole.
3. Refit the blade, adjust the tension and make sure that the worktable is set at the correct angle.
4. Switch on the power and feed the wood into the blade so that the line of cut is slightly to the waste side of the drawn line.
5. Remove the waste and unhitch the blade.

scroll saw or fretsaw multiple cutting The process of stacking layers of plywood together and cutting a number of identical multiples at one and the same time. For example, if the project calls for two identical profiles, you sandwich two sheets of plywood together with pins or double-sided sticky tape, cut through both layers at the same time, and then ease the layers apart and remove the temporary fixings.

setting out The act of transferring the working drawings through to the face of the wood and making initial cuts. See *pencils* and *pencil-press transferring*.

sharpening tools All your cutting and edge tools need to be sharp. Ideally, you need a grindstone to reshape the bevel on a chipped or blunt edge, and an oilstone for honing and rubbing down to a keen fine edge.

 Be warned: Because blunt chisels are difficult and awkward to use, they are more dangerous than sharp chisels (FIG. G-16).

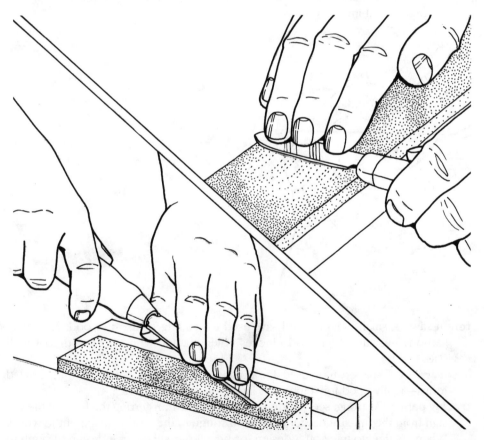

G-16 (top) To sharpen a knife, hold the blade at a flat angle to the oilstone and carefully draw it backwards and push it forwards. Turn the blade over and repeat the procedure. (bottom) Hold the chisel bevel-down, adjust the angle to suit, and then draw it backwards and push it forwards.

softwood Timber from a coniferous tree. It doesn't follow that softwoods are any softer or any easier to work than so-called hardwoods. We favor using two light-colored hardwoods—lime/linden because it is so easy to carve and shape and beech because it takes a crisp, hard-cornered finish.

steel ruler A long, flexible tape measure, usually 6–10 feet long. Very useful for measuring long runs and around curved profiles.

stick tools Any item you might have around the workshop that you can use to support sandpaper might be termed a *stick tool*. We tend to use such things as lolly sticks, broken hacksaw blades, and bits of dowel. In use, the sandpaper is held in place with pins or sticky tape, and then held and used like a file.

straight saws Straight, flat-bladed woodworking saw, rather than a coping or fretsaw. See *tenon saw, cross-cut,* and *gents.*

templates A pattern or shape cut from thin sheet wood or cardboard. In use, the template is set flat-down on the wood and drawn around to reproduce a number of identical images (FIG. G-17).

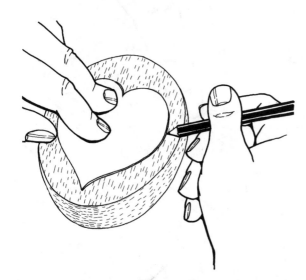

G-17 Set the template flat-down on the workpiece, align it with registration points, and carefully draw around it with a pencil.

tenon saw A small brass-backed saw used for cutting joints, plywood, and small sections—usually about 14–16 inches in length, and with 12–14 teeth to 1 inch (FIG. G-18).

T-square A T-shaped tool used for drawing and setting out large right angled forms—really good for setting out large sheets of plywood.

tracing paper A strong, see-through paper used for transferring the lines of the design from the full-size master drawing through to the working face of the wood. When it's time to trace off a design, or pencil-press transfer a design through to the wood, always make sure that the tracing paper is well secured with tabs of masking tape. See *pencils* and *pencil-press transferring.*

try square Sometimes called a square, a try square is a tool used to test work for straightness and for 90° angles (FIG. G-19).

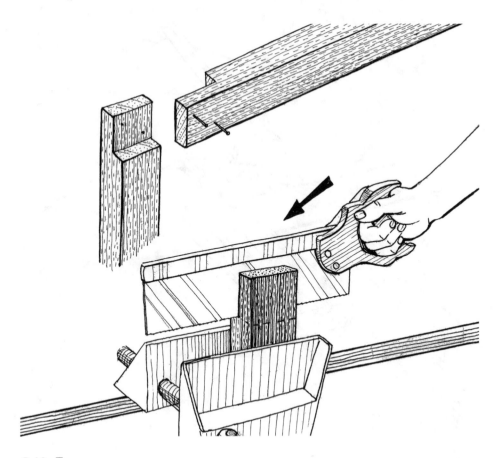

G-18 Tenon saw.

varnish In the context of this book—meaning woodwork that is to be painted and decorated with acrylic paints—it's best to use a clear or golden, high-shine polyurethane varnish.

vice A bench-mounted screw clamp, used for holding and securing the wood while it is being worked.

whittling From the Anglo-Saxon word *thwitan*, meaning to cut and pare with a small knife. Many woodworking projects involve a small amount of whittling: Curves are cut back, dowel-ends are rounded, and so on. Currently we use a craft knife, a scalpel, and a penknife.

wood Timber and boards are the basic woodwork material. We favor using beech, lime/linden and jelutong. When you are buying your wood, avoid material that looks to be stained, knotty, split, twisted, or sappy. Spend time searching around for a piece that allows for the smallest possible amount of cutting waste. When we describe such-and-such a piece of wood as being *prepared*, we mean a piece that has been planed on all edges and faces. Although we usually spec-

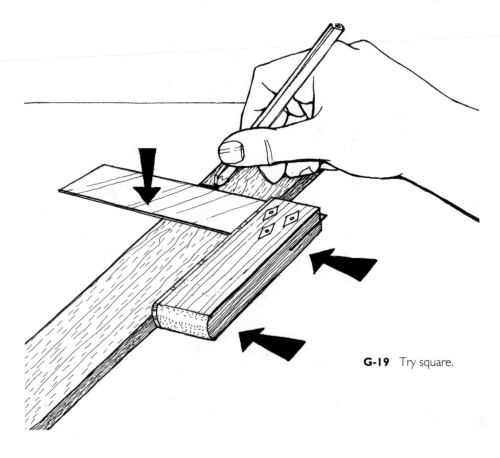

G-19 Try square.

ify wood that has been sized in multiples of ¼ inch (meaning ¼ inch, ½ inch, ¾ inch, and so on), and although we usually order wood to a preferred finished size, the norm is for wood to be planed to a nominal size. For example a piece of 3-×–1-inch section wood might actually measure 2⅞ inches × ⅞ inch.

workbench A workbench might be just about anything from a worksurface out in the garage through to the kitchen table, a side table in a spare room, or a purpose built woodworkers bench. The workbench needs to be strong, stable, at the correct height, clean, and fitted with a vice.

working drawings The scaled, measured, or full-size drawing, from which all other measurements are taken. See *designing*.

working face In the context of this book, the working face is the best side of the wood, the side that shows, the side that is going to be on view once the project has been put together.

working height Although of course it's important that all woodworkers are at a good comfortable height to the working surface—not too much stooping, stretching or straining—it's especially important for kids. We say this because if the child is working at the wrong height, then most likely he or she will be using the tools in a way that is both inefficient and dangerous. It's a good idea to set each child up with their own individual dias. This small portable platform doesn't have to be anything fancy, just a few old planks nailed or screwed across a couple of blocks—no more or less than a stable, non-wobble surface to bring the child up to the correct working height. Bear in mind that the child's elbows need to be higher than the workbench.

workout paper Paper on which all the pre-project notes, details, and sketches are worked out prior to actually getting to making marks on the wood. We use a hardcover sketch book for all the initial designs and small details, gridded papers, and lengths of end-of-roll printers paper/decorators paper for the full-size patterns. Make tracings so as to save all your patterns for the next time around.

I
Launching
out

Making a
bathtub yacht:

A small solid-wood and dowel matchbox-sized boat—just perfect for bathtime fun.

Primary techniques:

Compass work, sawing, drilling, sanding, scissor cutting, and painting.

Age level: 7–8

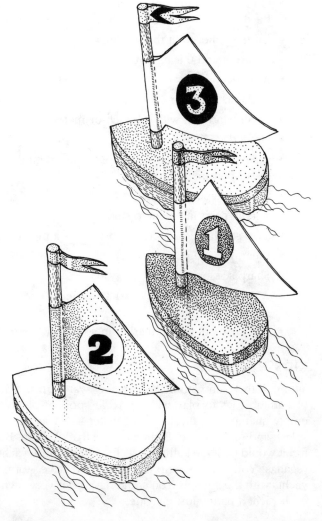

WOODS

For each yacht:

- A 3-inch length of prepared wood, 1½ inches wide by ¾ inch thick. (Best to use an easy-to-work knot-free wood like lime/linden, sycamore, or white pine.) If your workshop is full of off-cuts, you could make yachts all different shapes and sizes.
- A 3¼-inch length of ⅛-inch-diameter dowel for the mast. Throw-away woods (such as popsicle sticks) are really good, but wash and dry them before use.

TOOLS & MATERIALS

- Small, straight, flat-bladed saw
- Workbench with vice
- One 1¼-inch-long roundhead screw and a screwdriver to fit. The screw must be slender enough to pass through a ⅛-inch-diameter hole.
- Large washer to fit the screw
- Workout and tracing paper
- A small compass
- G-clamp
- Small hand drill with a ⅛-inch-diameter bit
- Graded sandpaper
- A selection of found stick tools to use with the sandpaper (bits of flat waste to support the sandpaper)
- Masking tape
- Acrylic paint in colors to suit
- Two soft-haired watercolor brushes—a medium-broad and a fine-point
- Clear, high-shine varnish
- Sharp scissors
- A piece of colored sticky-backed shelf- cover plastic sheet at 2 × 5 inches for each yacht.
- A permanent felt-tip marker in a color to contrast the plastic sheet

KIDS'-EYE VIEW

Sitting in the bath with the hot steamy water up to your chin and a good selection of bathtub toys to play with—a large sponge, plenty of soap, a rubber duck, an empty shampoo bottle to squirt water—and as much time as you like to splish splash and play around! Bathtime is really good fun. But just think how much more fun it would be if the bathtub was full of miniature yachts. You could have races and regattas. You could stir up the water and have storms. You could dive-bomb the yachts with the sponge. You could have your very own bathtub yacht club and give each yacht a name. Just imagine!

Made from little pieces of softwood and fitted out with plastic sails and dowel masts, these yachts are so easy to make that you could have four or five put together in the space of one rainy afternoon. While you are at it, you might just as well make a couple of yachts for your mom and dad; if you don't, they are only going to play with yours!

CAREGIVERS' GUIDE

Making Time and Skill Level—Although this project is relatively easy, its smallness might well pose problems of just how to hold the wood secure while it is being worked. As long as the child knows how to use a small saw and a hand drill, (and with a little bit of help), a keen, well-motivated 7- or 8-year-old will have these little yachts made and varnished at a rate of about one an hour.

Cautions and Adult Help—Although the techniques are straightforward, you might need to show your kids how to hold the wood secure in the vice. That said, if you keep the children well supplied with off-cuts of the correct length, they should be able to take it from there.

Be Warned—No matter how watchful you are, enthusiastic can't-wait-to-get-the-boat-in-the-water kiddies are almost certainly going to graze their knuckles on one or all of the edged tools. So best be on stand-by, ready with a swab and a good supply of band-aids.

GETTING DOWN TO WORK

1. Have a look at the project picture (on page 1), the working drawing (FIG. 1-1), and the design template (FIG. 1-2), and see how the little yacht is made up from four components—the hull, the mast, the sail, and the flag. Note how the shape of the hull, as seen in plan view, has been worked out with a compass. See also the way the sticky-backed plastic sheet is wrapped around the mast so that the sticky faces meet.

2. Make sure that your 3-inch length of prepared 1½-inch-wide, ¾-inch-thick wood is in good condition. Because it is a relatively small piece of wood, it needs to be free from splits and knots.

3. Pencil-label the 3-inch × 1½-inch face of the wood "top deck" and one or other of the ends "front" or "prow."

4. Draw the design up to full size, make a tracing of the yacht as seen in the plan view, and then pencil-press transfer the traced lines through to the "top deck" face of the wood (FIG. 1-3, top). Shade in the waste areas that need to be cut away, and use the ruler and try square to draw in a centerline. Establish the position of the mast at a point about ¾ inch along from the prow (FIG. 1-3, bottom). If necessary, use the compass to strengthen and/or modify the shapes of the stem and stern.

5. With the wood clamped firmly down on a piece of scrap wood on the bench, bore out the mast hole using the hand drill and the ⅛-inch-diameter bit. Make sure that the drill hole is at right angles to the top deck (FIG. 1-4, left).

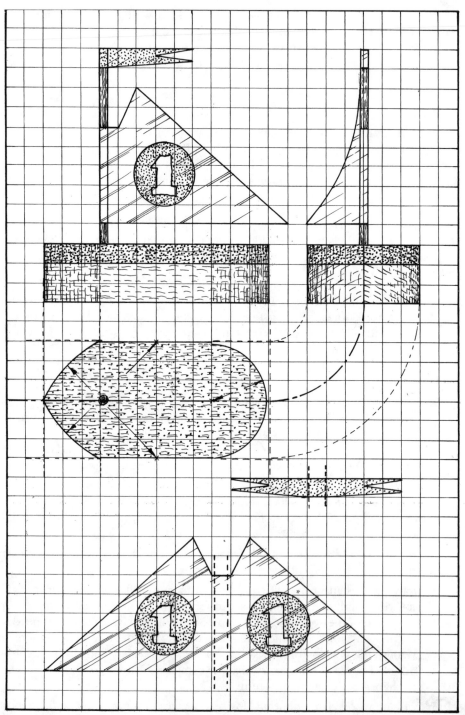

1-1 Working Drawing. Scale: 4 grid squares to 1 inch. The yacht measures 3 inches long, 1½ inches wide, and ¾ inch deep. Note the run of the grain and the details of mast, sail and flag.

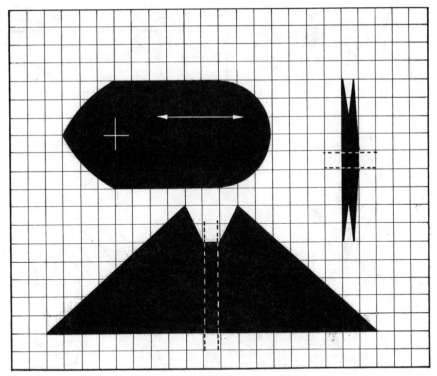

1-2 Design Template—The scale is 4 grid squares to 1 inch. Top: the plan view of the hull; right: the flag; bottom: the complete pattern for the wrap-around sail.

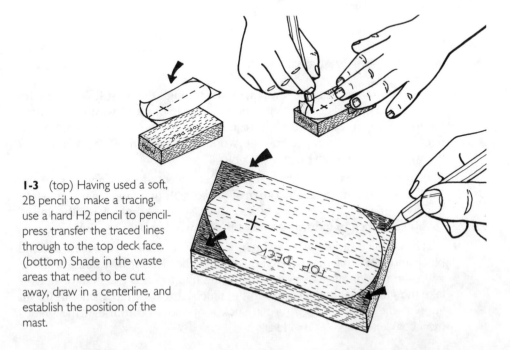

1-3 (top) Having used a soft, 2B pencil to make a tracing, use a hard H2 pencil to pencil-press transfer the traced lines through to the top deck face. (bottom) Shade in the waste areas that need to be cut away, draw in a centerline, and establish the position of the mast.

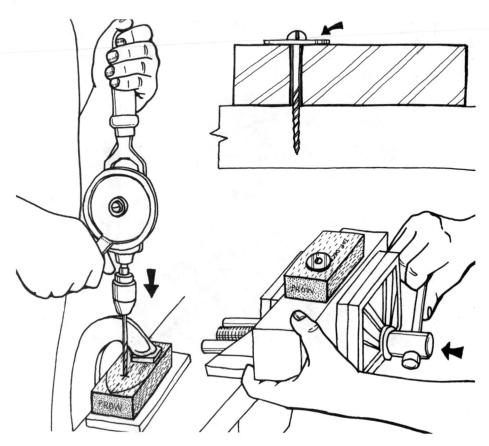

1-4 (left) Bore out the mast hole. (top right) Pass the screw through the washer and on through the mast hole. (bottom right) Secure the block in the jaws of the vice so that the top face of the waste block is slightly above the vice/bench line.

6. Pass the screw through the washer, down through the mast hole. Screw-fix the workpiece top-side-uppermost onto a sizable block of waste wood (FIG. 1-4, top right), and secure the block in the jaws of the vice (FIG. 1-4, bottom right). If you want to reposition the workpiece, slacken off the screw, turn the wood, and then retighten the screw.

7. With the wood screwed down and held at an easy-to-saw angle, take the small saw and remove each corner of waste with two tangential cuts. Hold the saw upright, and—working at a steady easy pace—try to keep the line of cut about ¹⁄₁₆ inch to the waste side of the drawn line (FIG. 1-5, right).

8. When you have sliced away the bulk of the waste, remove the screw and the block and reposition the roughed-out form in the vice. Now working with the grain—in this instance, from the side of the hull towards the stem or stern— take the graded sandpaper and rub the little shape down to a smooth finish. Support the sandpaper with a flat stick tool and work through the grades from coarse to fine (FIG. 1-5, left).

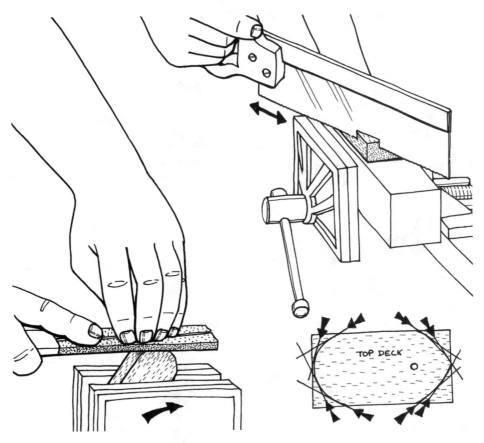

1-5 (top right) Use the saw to remove the corners of waste. (bottom) Use the graded sandpaper to rub the sawn areas down to a smooth, curved finish, as shown.

9. When you are happy with the shape and finish of the hull, take the 3¼-inch length of ⅛-inch-diameter dowel, and carefully tap it down into the mast hole. Ideally, it should be a tight push-fit (FIG. 1-6).

10. Now, having wiped away the dust and moved to the area set aside for painting, cover the sides of the hull with masking tape, leaving a ¼-inch-wide uncovered strip around the top edge. Wrap a strip of tape around the bottom of the mast. Take the fine-point brush and a good bold color—preferably one to contrast your sail material—and paint the top deck and the ¼-inch-wide band that runs around the top edge of the hull (FIG. 1-7).

11. When the acrylic paint is completely dry, remove the masking tape, hang the little boat up by its mast, and give it a couple of all-over coats of clear varnish.

12. While the varnish is drying, trace off the shape of the sail and the little flag, and pencil-press transfer the drawn shapes through to the backing-paper side of the plastic sheet. Use the scissors to carefully cut the shapes out (FIG 1-8).

1-6 Gently tap the dowel down through the drilled mast hole. If you have to use a heavy general-purpose claw hammer like the one shown, be sure to make small lightweight taps so as not to split the wood.

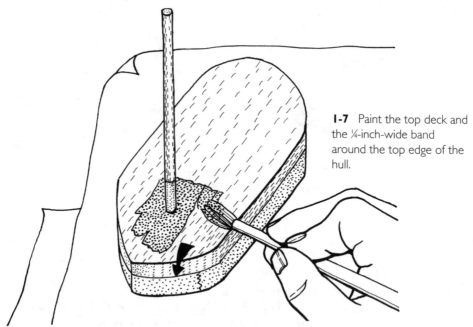

1-7 Paint the top deck and the ¼-inch-wide band around the top edge of the hull.

13. Using the felt-tip marker, give the sail a name, number, or image.

14. Having made sure that the varnish is dry, peel the backing paper off the sail to just over the halfway mark. Set the centerline of the sail on the mast at a point about ¼ inch up from the deck. Now slowly peel away the paper; at the same time, carefully wrap the two halves of the sail round the mast, and stick them together face to face (FIG. 1-9). Repeat this procedure with the little flag, and your yacht is ready to be launched!

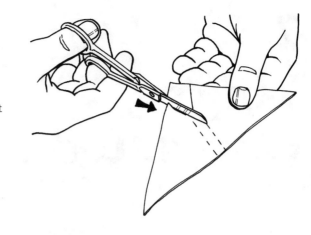

1-8 Cut the large outer shape first and then the stepped details.

1-9 Peel off half of the backing paper, place and align the sticky-backed plastic on the mast, remove the rest of the backing paper, and stick the two halves of the sail together.

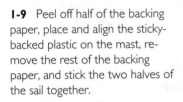

WATCHPOINTS

If the child is very young and the sawing results in a jagged finish, you might want to rasp the hull before you sand it.

If possible, use a brass-backed, small-toothed, tenon or gents saw. Such a tool is relatively lightweight and easy to handle. It's one of the most useful all-purpose saws.

If the yacht is to survive regular bathtime water bombings, you will need to varnish the whole thing generously.

If you do decide to use small off-cuts, avoid oily exotic hardwoods, as they are sometimes difficult to work and unpleasant to handle.

2
King's castellated castle

Making a model castle:

A flat-pack castle with battlements, a portcullis, and coats of arms.

Primary techniques:

Fretting, using a tenon saw, drilling, slot jointing, screwing, sanding, potato printing, and painting.

Age level: 8–9

WOODS

- A sheet of best-quality ¼-inch-thick birch-faced multicore plywood at 48 × 48 inches. This allows a generous amount for spare, just in case you mess up.

    Note: If you are trying to cut costs, you could buy small off-cuts. But if you want to make several projects, buying in bulk is the cheapest way. Buying a 48-x-48-inch half sheet (or better still, buying a 96-x-48-inch whole sheet) is the best way of buying the plywood.

- A 60-inch length of prepared 1-x-1-inch-square section of straight-grained knot-free pine. This allows for spare and cutting waste.

TOOLS AND MATERIALS

- Coping saw and a pack of spare blades
- Workbench with a vice
- One sheet each of tracing and workout paper large enough for one whole castle wall
- Large, general-purpose saw
- Flat-bladed saw like a tenons or a gents
- Two small G-clamps
- Pencil, ruler, straightedge, and try square
- Hand drill with a selection of bits to fit
- Graded sandpaper
- Acrylic paints in various colors
- Two paintbrushes, a broad and a fine-point
- Two large potatoes
- Long-bladed serrated kitchen knife and a cutting board (for the potatoes)
- Sixteen ½-inch-long roundhead brass screws (for the battlements)
- Twelve ⅜-inch-long, roundhead brass screws (for the portcullis runners)
- Screwdriver to fit the screws
- White PVA wood glue
- Clear high-shine varnish
- One 12-inch length of ⅛-inch-diameter cord
- Two colored wooden beads at about ½-inch diameter, with holes large enough to take the cord

KIDS'-EYE VIEW

When I was a kid of about 8 years old, I was given a plywood castle. My brother and I used to set it up on a heap of damp sand, and then we shaped and modeled the sand to make a moat, roads, and underground tunnels. As I remember, most of our castle games had to do with Robin Hood. My brother would stand his soldiers on the battlements and in and around the earthworks, and then we would bombard the whole thing with little balls of damp sand. As the game progressed and we were joined by the girls next door, we introduced other toys—cars, farmyard animals, and dolls. By the end of the day we were usually in a terrible mess—with most of our toys buried and sand in our ears, up our noses, and just about everywhere else. It was great fun! So what are you waiting for? The sooner you get the castle built, the sooner you can get started with the siege and the bombardment!

CAREGIVERS' GUIDE

Making Time and Skill Level—This is one of those projects that looks much more complicated than it really is. Certainly there is a lot of precise measuring and sawing that is best checked by an adult, but as for the rest, it's all relatively easy and straightforward. If you have the space and the tools, it would be a great idea if you could spread the work load around and have the whole family/team/club helping. One wall per woodworker would be about right.

With a little bit of help, the average 8- to 9-year-old could have the castle made, painted, and out in the yard in the space of a weekend. Your kids could start on Saturday morning, decorate on Sunday, and have the castle full of soldiers by Monday. That can't be bad!

Note: Although the castle can be dismantled for flat-pack storage, it is a tricky, strong-wrist procedure that is best managed by an adult. That said, if you want to go for a castle that can easily be taken apart by the kids, make the slots wider, longer, and generally oversize.

Cautions and Adult Help—The various stages of the project are straightforward, but the initial setting out does require a bit of planning. This is not to say that the design is overly complicated, only that the castellations and the slots need to be very carefully measured, marked, and set out. If you or the child have any worries about how the sides fit and slot together, be sure to iron out the problems at the start of the project by building a mock-up prototype with sheets of carton cardboard.

Be Warned—When you are positioning the slots and cutting the castellations, measure twice and cut once. It's very easy to make a mess-up and cut away two neighboring squares, so it's a good idea to shade in the areas that need to be cut away.

GETTING DOWN TO WORK

1. Have a look at the project picture (page 10), the working drawing (FIG. 2-1) and the design templates (FIGS. 2-2 and 2-3), and see how the castle is made up from four near-identical walls, a sliding portcullis-door, four battlement strips, and various bits and pieces to make the door tracks/runners. Note such primary details as the 1-x-1-inch size of the castellations, the way the walls slot together at the corners, the printed "stone" pattern, the printed point-top windows, and the way the portcullis is raised and lowered by a bead-end pull-cord.

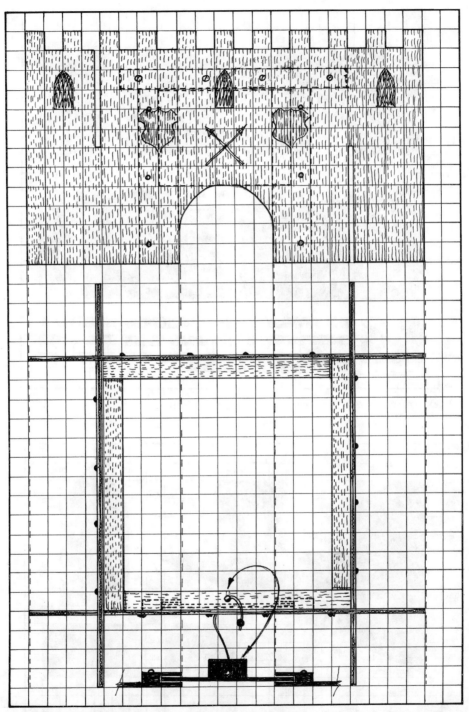

2-1 Working Drawing. At a scale of 1 grid square to 1 inch, the castle walls are 12 inches high and 21 inches long. Note the portcullis detail on the plan view.

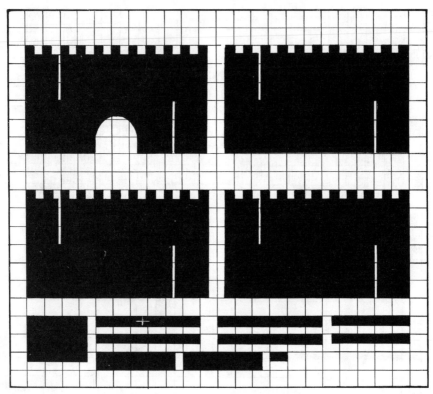

2-2 Design Template #1. The scale is 1 grid square to 2 inches.

2-3 Design Template #2. The scale of the details is 4 grid squares to 1 inch. (From left: the castellations, the window profile, and the two potato-print stone block sizes.)

2. Study your wood. If there are difficult-to-work problems like splits, stains, and loose knots, then look for another piece.

3. With the sheet of ¼-inch-thick plywood, use the pencil, measure, try square, and straightedge to set out the four 21-inch-long 12-inch-high rectangles that make up the four walls. Label one wall DOOR, the best face of all four walls FRONT, and the top edges TOP. When you have double-checked that the walls are the correct size and crisply square, carefully cut the four walls down to size with the saw.

4. Use the pencil, ruler, and try square to set out the 1-x-1-inch module/grid that makes up the castellations. Measure 1 inch down from the top edge, and then set the resultant 1-inch-wide strip with 21 1-inch-wide step-offs. From left to right along the top edge, number the step-offs from 1 through to 21. Shade in the even-numbered waste squares on all four walls (FIG. 2-4, left).

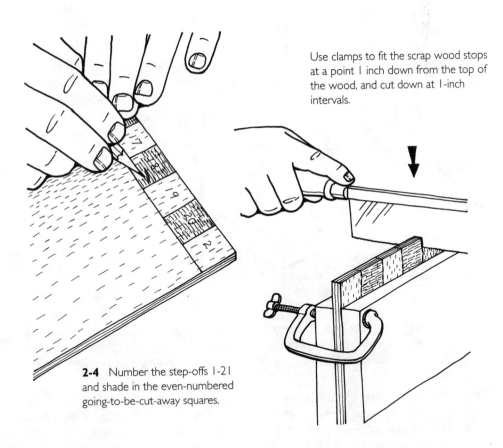

Use clamps to fit the scrap wood stops at a point 1 inch down from the top of the wood, and cut down at 1-inch intervals.

2-4 Number the step-offs 1-21 and shade in the even-numbered going-to-be-cut-away squares.

5. Set out the size and shape of the doorway, the size and position of the corner slots, and so on.

6. Working with one wall at a time—secure the wood in the vice, use the G-clamps to fit scrap wood stops 1 inch down from the top of the wood, and

use the tenon saw to work along the top edge, cutting down all the 1-inch-long vertical lines that set out the width of the castellations. Work at a steady pace, trying all the while to keep the cuts straight, to stop short when the teeth of the saw bit into the stop, and not to tear the wood (FIG. 2-4, right).

7. When you have cut down between the squares, and still using the stop as a guide, take the coping saw and carefully link up the bottom of paired cuts so that all the even-numbered squares fall away. Repeat this procedure with all four walls (FIG. 2-5). *Be warned*—It's very easy to accidentally cut away neighboring squares, so check every cut.

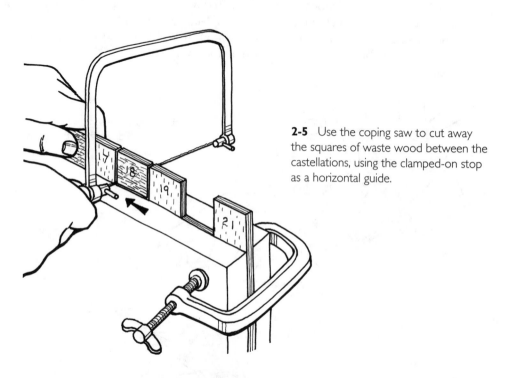

2-5 Use the coping saw to cut away the squares of waste wood between the castellations, using the clamped-on stop as a horizontal guide.

8. Having made sure that the corner slots are placed well, repeat the sawing procedure as already described, only this time, set the saw cuts ¼ inch apart and have them run halfway up/down the 12-inch height of the castle walls (FIG. 2-6, top).

9. When you have cut and worked the castellations and the corner slots, take the DOOR wall and use the coping saw to cut out the 5-inch-wide, 4-inch-high curve-topped doorway (FIG. 2-6, bottom). The rules of thumb when using the coping saw are:

   • Always have a pack of spare blades at the ready.

   • Make sure that the teeth are pointing away from the handle, that the blade is well-tensioned and that the workpiece is well-supported.

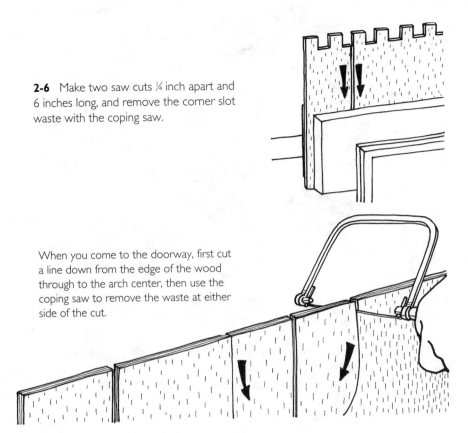

2-6 Make two saw cuts ¼ inch apart and 6 inches long, and remove the corner slot waste with the coping saw.

When you come to the doorway, first cut a line down from the edge of the wood through to the arch center, then use the coping saw to remove the waste at either side of the cut.

- Work at a steady, even pace so as not to twist the blade or rip the wood.
- Keep maneuvering both the saw and the workpiece so that the blade is always smoothly and timely presented with the line of next cut.
- Work very slightly to the waste side of the drawn line.

10. With the doorway nicely cut out, take the graded sandpaper and rub all the cut edges down to a slightly round-edged smooth-to-the-touch finish.

11. Use the pencil, ruler, and try square to set out the five ¼-inch-thick plywood parts of the sliding portcullis—the door piece at 7 × 5 inches, the two 9-inch-long 2-inch-wide strips, and the two 9-inch-long 1-inch-wide strips. Check the sizes off against the working drawing, cut them carefully to size with the straight saw, and sand to a smooth finish.

12. Look at the working drawing again (page 13) and notice how two strips are fitted at either side of the portcullis. The 1-inch-wide strip is sandwiched between the 2-inch-wide strip and the inside face of the wall, so that there is a 1-inch-wide, ¼-inch-thick slot at either side of the doorway. Drill pilot holes for the screws, and screw-fit the sliding strips into position in the following order:

    - Glue, position, and clamp the 2-inch-wide strip on top of the 1-inch-wide strip.

- Drill pilot holes through the 2-inch strip and fix the two strips together with screws (FIG. 2-7, left).
- Position the two-layer strip on the inside face of the doorway, and fix with screws driven through from the outside face of the wall (FIG. 2-7, right).

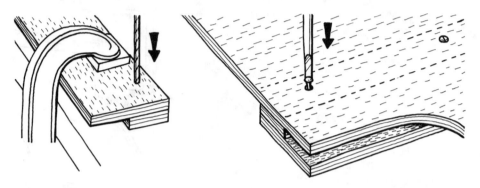

2-7 Glue the 2-inch-wide strip onto the 1-inch-wide strip, drill pilot holes, and fix with screws. Then drill pilot holes through the front wall, and screw the doorway strips in place.

13. Take the graded sandpaper and the 7-x-5-inch door piece and reduce the ¼-inch thickness on the two 5-inch edges by about ¹⁄₁₆ inch. Remove a skim from both faces until the portcullis is an easy sliding fit in the slot (FIG. 2- 8).

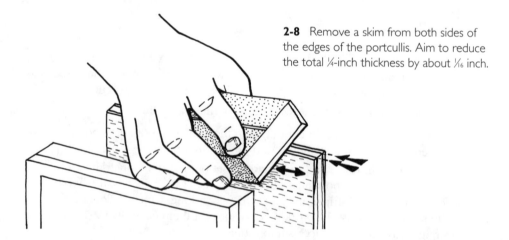

2-8 Remove a skim from both sides of the edges of the portcullis. Aim to reduce the total ¼-inch thickness by about ¹⁄₁₆ inch.

14. Having looked at the working drawing and noted how the 1-x-1-inch-square section battlement strips are placed, use the small saw to cut the wood into four identical 12-inch lengths.

15. Mark out the position of the strips on the inside castle walls, dribble a small amount of glue on the strip/wall—just enough to tack the strips in place—and carefully set them in position (FIG. 2-9, left).

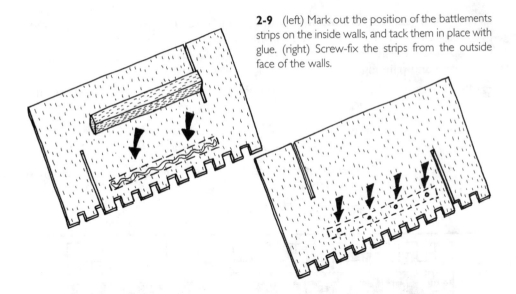

2-9 (left) Mark out the position of the battlements strips on the inside walls, and tack them in place with glue. (right) Screw-fix the strips from the outside face of the walls.

16. When the glue is dry, turn the walls over so that they are outside-face-up, drill pilot holes through the walls and into the strips, and then screw-fix with four roundhead screws (FIG. 2-9, right). If all is well, all you should be able to see of the screws is four round heads on the outside of each wall.

17. Take the portcullis/door sheet, and glue-fix a little block of wood to the top inside edge. Drill two ⅛-inch-diameter holes, one down through the block and another through the wall strip at a point just above the doorway (FIG. 2-10).

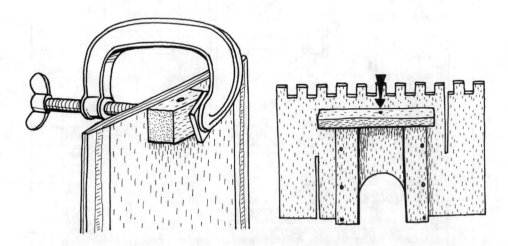

2-10 (left) Glue-fix the 2-inch-long 1-x-1-inch-square section block to the top inside edge of the portcullis. (right) Run a ⅛-inch hole through the battlement strip at a point just above the center of the doorway.

18. When you consider the woodwork finished—that is, when the castle comes together for a good fit with all edges and faces being rubbed down to a smooth finish—wipe off all the dust, and move to the area set aside for printing and painting.

19. Have a good long look at the design templates (FIGS. 2-2 and 2-3) and the painting grids (FIGS. 2-11 and 2-12). Begin printing as follows:

    • Cut the potato in half. Slice away the side face so that you have two printing stamps—one at 1 × ¾-inches and the other at 1½ × ¾ inches (FIG. 2-13).

    • Scoop away a small part of the center of the printing face. (See the dotted lines on FIG. 2-3, bottom right).

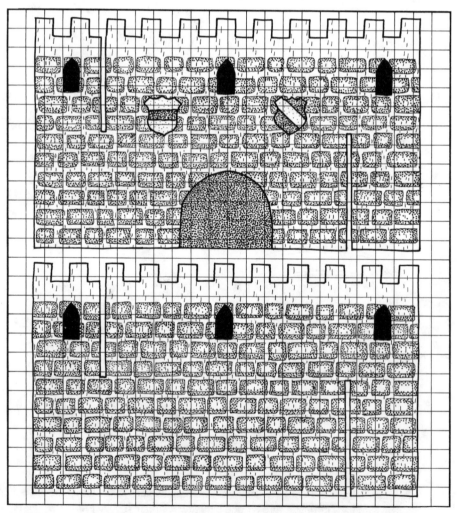

2-11 Painting grid #1. The scale is 1 grid square to 1 inch.

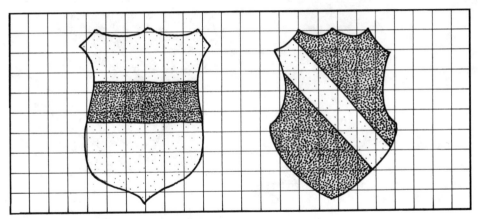

2-12 Painting grid #2. The scale is 4 grid squares to 1 inch.

- Place the walls best-face-up on the worksurface. Starting 2 inches down from the top of the castellations, use a pencil and ruler to set the wood out from top to bottom with a series of 1-inch-apart guidelines.

- Brush a small amount of nonrunny stone-colored acrylic paint (yellow-orange or brown-orange) on a piece of scrap ply. Press the potato stamps in the paint, and swiftly print the walls off with a stone-block pattern.

- For best effect, set the horizontal mortar spaces between the stones carefully on the guideline, and keep the vertical spaces staggered (FIG. 2-14, top).

2-13 Use a kitchen knife and a cutting board to slice the potatoes to shape.

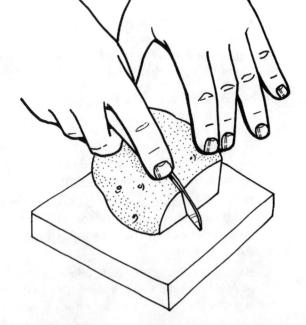

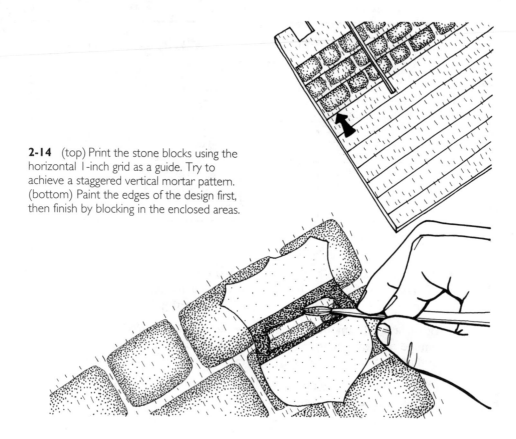

2-14 (top) Print the stone blocks using the horizontal 1-inch grid as a guide. Try to achieve a staggered vertical mortar pattern. (bottom) Paint the edges of the design first, then finish by blocking in the enclosed areas.

- Keep the paint reservoir topped up, and work at a swift pace so that overall the printed repeat image looks to be slightly blurred and textured. Note that the 4-inch top-to-bottom strip at each end of the walls need to be set out with guidelines and printed on both sides (FIG. 2-14, bottom).

20. When the printed stone block pattern is dry, repeat the potato printing procedure to print the windows. Cut and print as already described, only this time, use matte black paint and cut and shape the potato so as to achieve a crisp point-topped window image (FIG. 2-3, bottom right). Print the windows over the stone blocks—three on the outside face of each wall, and two on the back face for the corner towers.

21. Draw your chosen shield or coat-of-arms motif to size, trace off the design, and pencil-press transfer the traced lines through to the walls. Use the fine-point brush and the colors of your choice to block-in and hand paint the design (FIG. 2-14).

22. Having masked off the side edges of the 7-x-5-inch door piece/portcullis, paint it bright red on both sides (FIG. 2-15, top left). Wait for the paint to dry, and give the whole castle a couple of thin coats of varnish.

23. Finally, thread a length of cord through the hole in the top-of-door block and through the hole in the wall. Slide the portcullis door in place, thread on the wooden beads, and knot off the ends of the cord (FIG. 2-15 bottom). The castle is finished and ready for the great battle and bombardment!

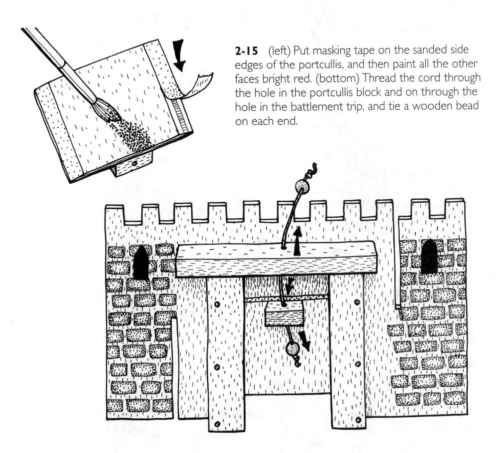

2-15 (left) Put masking tape on the sanded side edges of the portcullis, and then paint all the other faces bright red. (bottom) Thread the cord through the hole in the portcullis block and on through the hole in the battlement trip, and tie a wooden bead on each end.

WATCHPOINTS

If you can use a scroll saw, you could speed up the making process and go for more rounded and worn-looking forms.

You could modify the design and build it with a hinged drawbridge, or as an Alamo-type western fort or even a log fort.

3
Monkey memo

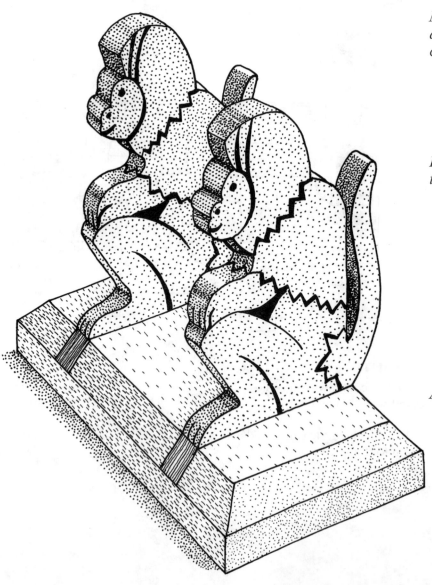

Making a desk-top monkey cardholder:

A letters-and-note holder with monkey imagery.

Primary techniques:

Fretting, sawing, using a chisel to cut a housing/ housed slot, using a plane, sanding, gluing, and painting.

Age level:

10–11

WOODS

- For the base, a piece of prepared ¾-inch-thick, easy-to-work wood, 4 inches long and 2 inches wide. Use a smooth-grained, non-split, knot-free wood like white pine, American whitewood, maple, or parana pine.
- A sheet of best-quality ¼-inch-thick birch-faced multicore plywood at 6½ × 3 inches. Try to cut the wood so that the grain is running from top to bottom of the monkey.

TOOLS & MATERIALS

- Small, flat-bladed saw
- Fretsaw with a pack of spare blades
- Bird's-mouth cutting board and a clamp to use with the fretsaw
- Workbench with a vice
- Bench hook sawing board
- Marking knife (you can use a pocketknife)
- Pencil and ruler
- Small, bevel-edged chisel (best if it's slightly narrower than the ¼-inch-wide groove)
- One sheet each of workout and tracing paper
- Try square
- Marking gauge
- Small hand plane
- White PVA wood glue
- Graded sandpaper
- Masking tape
- Modeling clay (small amount)
- Acrylic paints (orange-brown and black)
- Two watercolor brushes, a broad and a fine-point
- Drawing pins/thumbtacks
- High-shine varnish

KIDS'-EYE VIEW

According to Charles Darwin, monkeys and humans share the same roots. If I understand this correctly, it means that if we were to travel back in time, you, me, and the monkey would have the same grandfather. Hmm . . . does that make us all country cousins?

Next time you visit the zoo, take a look at the monkeys and see how they always draw a crowd. It's great fun watching them jumping up and down, grinning, chattering, and feeding. (I also enjoy watching the monkeys—ha!) But no more monkeying around. It's time to get down to work. The memo/cardholder is a clever idea.

The two little African Hamadryas Baboons—what a name!—sit side by side and are cut and mounted in such a way that the springy curve of their tails is enough to grip and hold a memo, a card, a photo, a ticket, or your pocket-money allowance . . .

CAREGIVERS' GUIDE

Making Time and Skill Level—Using a fretsaw is easy enough, but handling and using a chisel to cut a housing joint is something again. This is not to say that chisel work is any more complicated than using a saw; it is only that it's more dangerous. For this reason, show the children how to use the chisel, and then carefully watch them while they are cutting joints. I would say that an average 10- or 11-year-old will have this project three-parts made in a day.

Cautions and Adult Help—I think it fair to say that certain sharp-edged tools—like chisels and knives—are always going to be potentially dangerous. Make a slip with a piece of sandpaper, and the very worst you can do is graze a finger, but the same slip with a chisel is a different story altogether. This doesn't mean that you have to fret and fuss about a 10-year-old using a chisel, only that you have to do your best to carefully organize the child and the working area.

Using the chisel is safe enough as long as you hold the chisel with both hands, always keep both hands behind the blade, and always work away from your body. On no account should children be waving the chisel around or working towards the body, or working with a kid brother or sister at the other side of the workbench.

When guiding children in the use of a chisel, be sure the work is held secure, the chisel is sharp, and there are no hands or onlookers between the child doing the work and the wood being cut. The best advice is for you to cut one housing joint, and then closely watch and help while the child cuts the other one.

Be Warned—sooner or later the chisel will slip, so just make sure that your hands and the child's hands are well behind the thrust of the blade, and always see to it that there is a first-aid kit in the workshop.

GETTING DOWN TO WORK

1. Study the project picture (on page 24) and the working drawings and design template (FIG. 3-1) to see how the project is made up from three component parts—the slotted base and the two monkey cutouts. The scale is 4 grid squares to 1 inch. The ¾-inch-thick stand measures 3½ inches long and 2 inches wide, while the total base-to-top-of-monkey height is a little under 3½ inches. The monkeys are set 1½ inches apart, with the slot between the monkey's tail and back no wider than the thickness of a single saw cut. See also the way the two housing/housed grooves run across the width of the stand, and how the two profiles are cut, worked, and fitted in the grooves so that the edge of the plywood runs out at the end of the grooves to finish flush with the beveled edge of the base.

3-1 Working Drawing and Design Templates. At a scale of 4 grid squares to 1 inch, the monkey stands about 3½ inches high, 3 ½ inches wide, and 2 inches from front to back.

2. When you have a clear picture of just how the project needs to be made and put together, draw the monkey design up to full size, make a tracing, and pencil-press transfer the traced design through to the multicore plywood. Have the grain running from head through to base (FIG. 3-2).

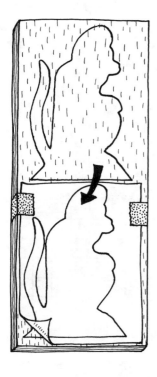

3-2 Pencil-press transfer the traced design through to the plywood so that the surface grain is running from top to toe.

3. Take the 4-inch length of ¾-inch wood, and use the pencil ruler and try square to set out all the details of the base. The finished base needs to be 3½ inches long, with the grooves being set in from the end of the base by ¾ inch. Label the grooved face TOP.

4. When you have drawn out all the details of the base, take the try square and the marking knife and set the pencil-drawn width of the grooves out with deeply scored lines. Make sure that the width of the scored lines occurs within the waste of the groove (FIG. 3-3, right).

5. Clamp the bench hook in the vice, hold the workpiece firmly against the bench-hook stop, and use the tenon or gents saw to carefully cut the wood to length. Make sure that you hold the saw upright so that the cut edge is square and at right angles to the TOP face (FIG. 3-4).

6. Use the pencil, ruler, square and marking gauge to set out the ¼-inch width of the bevel (FIG. 3-5), and then set the wood in the vice and use the small plane to run the beveled edge around the wood (FIG. 3-6). Be very careful not to cut too deeply or to split the end-grain off at the corners. Work from end-to-end along the length of the wood, and from end-to-center on the width.

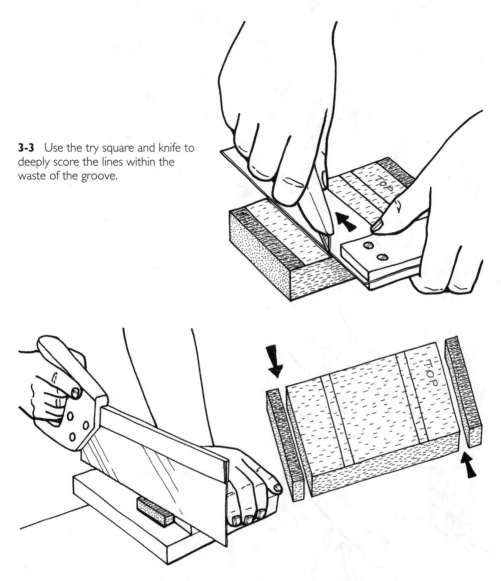

3-3 Use the try square and knife to deeply score the lines within the waste of the groove.

3-4 Push the wood hard up against the bench hook, and hold the saw upright so that the cut edge is at right angles to the top face.

7. When you have cut the bevel to an angle of about 45 degrees, secure the wood with a clamp and, using the small saw, cut the grooves into a depth of ¼ inch (FIG. 3-7, left). Be sure to keep the cuts on the waste side of the scored lines so that the width of the cuts and the width of the between-cut waste add up to the total ¼-inch width of the groove. A strip of tape stuck on the side of the saw blade makes a good depth gauge, and supporting the saw blade against the side of a piece of scrap wood helps to keep the saw cuts at right angles to the top face (FIG. 3-7, right).

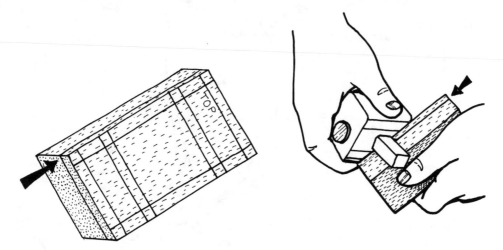

3-5 Use the marking gauge to set out the ¼-inch bevels that run along the length of the grain.

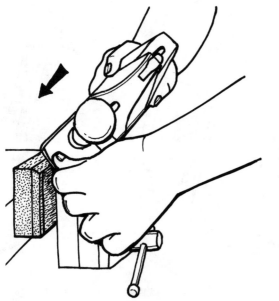

3-6 Set the wood in the vice and use the small plane to run the bevel around the top edge of the base.

8. With the width of the grooves now crisply set in with ¼-inch-deep saw cuts, secure the wood in the vice, take the small chisel in both hands—ideally, it should be slightly narrower than the groove—and skim off the groove waste with a series of carefully considered, upward-sloping paring cuts. Always hold the chisel in both hands, one hand guiding and the other pushing (FIG. 3-8). Work from edge-to-center on both grooves, and then turn the wood around in the vice and repeat the procedure from the other side. When you have cleared the groove from edge-to-center so that you are left with peaks

3-7 Secure the wood on the workbench and support the saw so that it is at right angles to the top face. Stick a strip of tape to the side of the saw blade to act as a depth gauge.

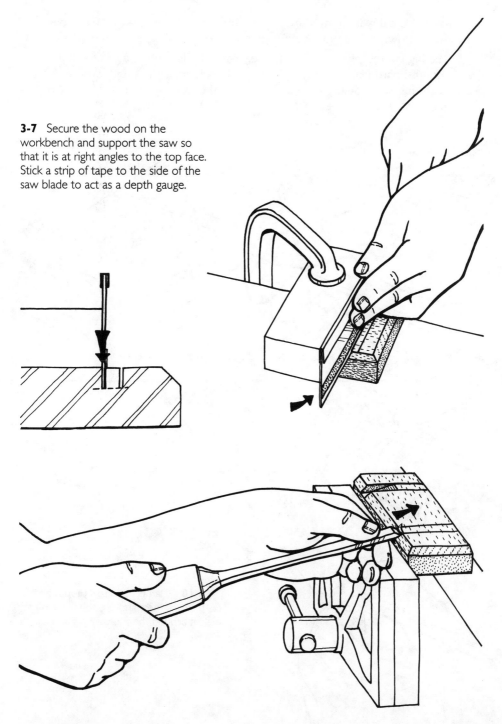

3-8 Hold the chisel with both hands—one guiding and the other pushing—and work from edge-to-center along both grooves.

of waste halfway along the grooves, hold the chisel flat-down and pare the waste down to a good level finish (FIG. 3-9).

9. Having cut the plywood into two easy-to-handle pieces, and with the bird's-mouth board clamped securely to the bench, take the plywood—all set out with the two monkey outlines—and use the fretsaw to cut out the two profiles (FIG. 3-10).

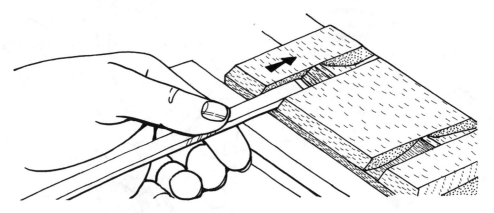

3-9 Hold the chisel flat-down and pare the waste down to a good level finish.

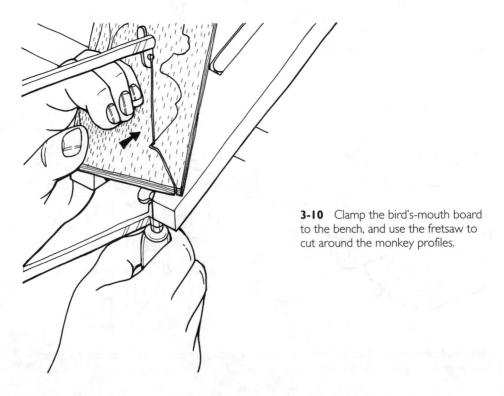

3-10 Clamp the bird's-mouth board to the bench, and use the fretsaw to cut around the monkey profiles.

The rules of thumb when using a fretsaw are:

- Make sure that the blade is well-tensioned.
- Hold the saw so that the blade runs through the wood at right angles to the face of the plywood.
- Work at steady pace so as not to tear the wood.
- Keep the wood moving so that the point of cut is as near as possible to the vertex of the bird's-mouth V.
- Work a little to the waste side of the drawn line.
- Keep the blade of the saw presented with the line of next cut.

10. When you have cut out the base and the two monkeys, take the graded sandpaper and rub the workpiece down to a smooth, slightly round-edged finish. At the point where the plywood runs out of the end of the groove, try to rub the plywood down so that it runs smoothly in with the bevel (FIG. 3-11).

11. Wipe away the dust, and move to the area set aside for painting. With the ¼-inch-wide bottom-of-monkey edge covered with masking tape and the whole thing supported on blobs of plastercine, use the following working order.

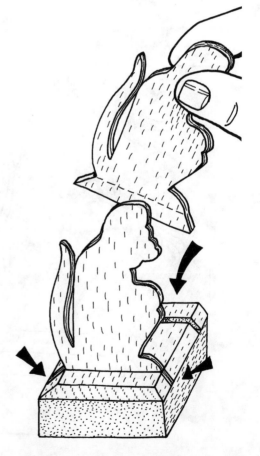

3-11 Sand the profiles down to a smooth-edged finish. Note how the bottom edge needs to run smoothly into the beveled edge of the base.

- Give the monkeys a couple of thin, all-over coats of acrylic orange-brown.
- Let the paint dry and give it a swift rubdown with a fine grade sandpaper.
- Pencil-press transfer the monkey design through to both sides of both monkeys (FIG. 3-1, top left).
- Pick out the design details with the black acrylic and the fine-point brush, and allow the project to dry.

12. When the paint is completely dry, carefully glue the two monkeys in their grooves. Make sure that they stand upright at right angles to the base, check that the tail slots are aligned, wipe away the excess glue, and put them to one side until the glue is completely set and dry.

13. When you are ready to varnish, first press thumbtacks into the base so that the varnish on the bottom edge doesn't dribble down and stick onto the worksurface (FIG. 3-12).

14. Lightly sand between coats, and lay on two or more thin coats of varnish. Let the varnish dry, remove the pins, and the job is done.

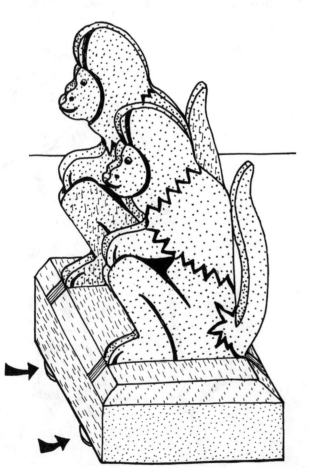

3-12 Use four thumbtacks to raise the base off from the worksurface, and then lay on the varnish.

WATCHPOINTS

If you have access to an electric scroll saw, you could sandwich the two pieces of plywood together with strips of double-sided tape and cut the two monkeys out at the same time. Working in this way it is possible to achieve two identical profiles.

Although you should be aiming for two identical monkeys, it does not matter too much if they are slightly different. Just make sure that the tail slots are more or less the same and in alignment with each other.

The African Hamadryas Baboon has a bright-red bottom—It could be a good fun feature of the design!

If you like the idea of the project, but are not so keen on having monkeys, you could go for another image.

4
Whizz whirler

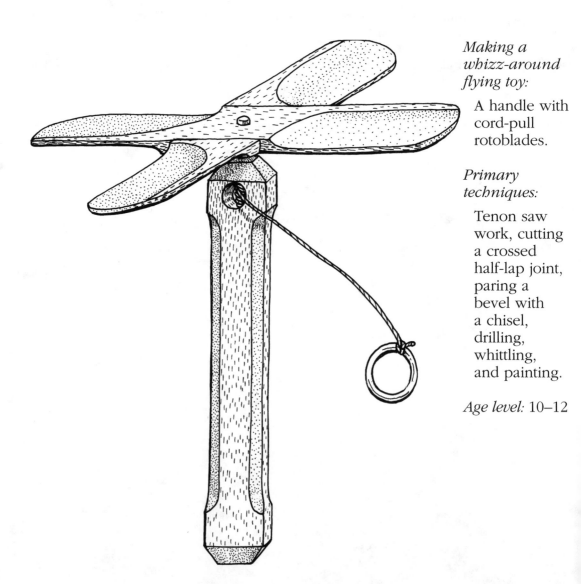

Making a whizz-around flying toy:

A handle with cord-pull rotoblades.

Primary techniques:

Tenon saw work, cutting a crossed half-lap joint, paring a bevel with a chisel, drilling, whittling, and painting.

Age level: 10–12

WOODS

- A 20-inch length of 1½-inch-wide, ¼-inch-thick, easy-to-carve lightweight wood (such as lime/linden or jelutong) for the rotoblades. This length allows for cutting waste.
- A 7-inch length of 1-x-1-inch-square section wood (such as lime, pine, or beech) for the launch-pad handle. This allows for a small amount of end waste.
- A 2-inch length of ¼-inch-diameter dowel.

TOOLS AND MATERIALS

- Coping saw
- Small brass-backed joint-cutting saw, like a tenon or a gents
- Small sharp block plane
- Workbench with a vice
- Bench hook sawing board
- Pencil and ruler
- One sheet of workout paper
- Marking gauge
- Try square
- Hand drill with bits at ½-inch, ⅜-inch, ¼-inch, and ⅛-inch diameter
- Bevel-edge chisel, 1 inch wide
- Craft knife
- Small clamp
- One strong, long, round-section bootlace (for the pull-cord)
- One metal curtain ring
- PVA wood glue
- Graded sandpaper
- Two paintbrushes, a broad and a fine-point
- Red acrylic paint
- Clear, high-shine varnish

KIDS'-EYE-VIEW

Kids love them, parents worry about them; whizz whirlers are dynamic, play-in-the-garden, sunshine toys. They are whizz-around flyers that have rotoblades like a helicopter; they spin through the air so fast that the colored blades blur together to make a spinning disc. Whizz whirlers are the perfect toy for the great outdoors.

Find a big open space, put on your flying goggles, set the rotoblade vane on its launch-pad handle, thread and wind the cord around the spindle, hold the launch handle at arm's length, give a sharp tug on the pull-cord and . . . three, two, one, zero . . . whizzzzz, varooooom, zoom! The whirler has lift-off!

CAREGIVERS' GUIDE

Making Time and Skill Level—This project involves the child in four primary woodworking procedures: cutting a crossed half-lap with a saw and chisel, cutting the chamfered handle with a chisel, whittling the rotoblades to shape, and drilling the pull-cord hole.

Although the individual working stages are relatively basic and straightforward, they do need to be worked with care. I would say that, with an adult on standby, a really keen and enthusiastic 11- to 12-year-old should be able to get the whirler made in a weekend.

Cautions and Adult Help—Chisels are a bit of a safety problem, so make sure that there is always an adult to help, advise, and guide.

There are three primary rules to follow when using a chisel:

1. The tool must be held in both hands, one holding and guiding, the other pushing.
2. The workpiece must always be held secure in a vice or with a clamp.
3. The chisel must be razor-sharp.

Be Warned—If the chisel is so blunt that it needs to be bullied into action, then it becomes dangerous.

Although whizz whirlers are good fun, they are also potentially dangerous. In use, hold the launch-pad handle at arm's length, wear safety goggles, play in a large, open space away from windows, power lines, and busy roads, and generally take care.

GETTING DOWN TO WORK

1. Have a look at the project picture (page 36) and the working drawing (FIG. 4-1) to see how the whirler is made up from four primary components—the two 8-inch lengths of the wood that make the crossed rotoblade, the 6-inch-long handle, and the spindle dowel. Note how each rotoblade has been sliced away and whittled to give it its characteristic airplane/helicopter prop twist. See also how the good-to-hold handle has been achieved by planing and chisel-paring the edges to a delicate chamfer.

2. Having drawn the design up to full size, check that your chosen wood is free from knots, splits, and stains, and make sure all your tools are in good condition. Then cut down the 20-inch length of 1½-inch-wide, ¼-inch-thick length of wood with the tenon saw so that you have two 10-inch lengths.

3. Using the pencil, ruler, marking gauge, and try square, set each 10-inch length out with end-to-end and side-to-side centerlines. This done, set the ruler down on the end-to-end centerline, and measure off 4 inches each side of the center point to give the total 8-inch prop length. Next, measure and mark ¾ inch in from each end to fix the compass points, and ¾ inch out each side of the center point to mark in the crossover point of the two lengths of wood (FIG. 4-2).

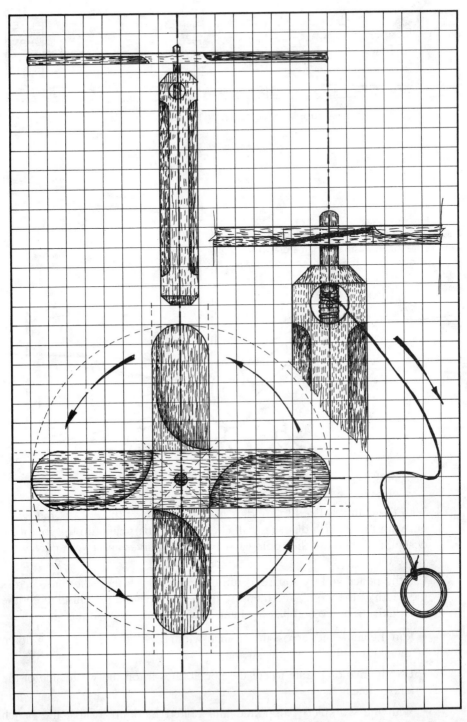

4-1 Working Drawing—(top and bottom). The scale is 2 grid squares to 1 inch (right). The scale is 4 grid squares to 1 inch—detail showing the pull-cord hole and pivot.

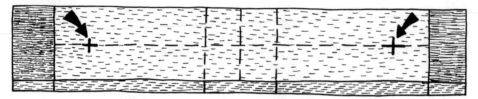

4-2 Shade in the end-of-wood areas of waste—note the compass center points for drawing the end-of-roto curves.

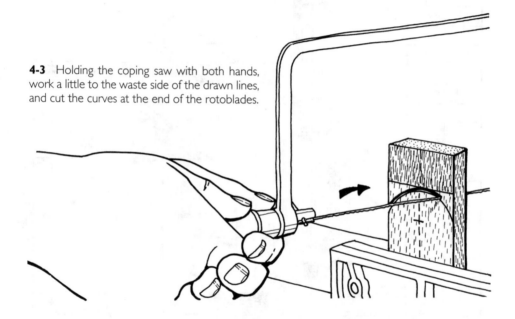

4-3 Holding the coping saw with both hands, work a little to the waste side of the drawn lines, and cut the curves at the end of the rotoblades.

4. With the compass fixed to a radius of ¾ inch, first set the ends of the wood out with the 1½-inch-diameter half-circle curves that make up the rotoblade design, and then use the coping saw to cut the curves and to clear away the waste (FIG. 4-3).

5. Use the pencil and try square to run the ¾-inch-out-from-center lines across the width of the wood, and then use the tenon saw and the chisel to cut the cross halving or crossed half-lap joint. The working procedure is:

   • Run the guidelines across the 1½-inch-width of the wood and ⅛ inch down the sides of the ¼-inch thickness.

   • Use the marking knife to cut the pencil lines in on the waste side of the drawn lines.

   • With the workpiece supported and butted hard up against the bench hook, use the tenon saw to make two cuts to establish the width and depth of the half-lap channel (FIG. 4-4).

- With the workpiece clamped to the bench, and being very careful not to cut too deep, use the chisel to pare away the waste and to lower the channel to a depth of ⅛ inch. Work the channel from one edge, and then turn the wood around and work in from the other (FIG. 4-5).

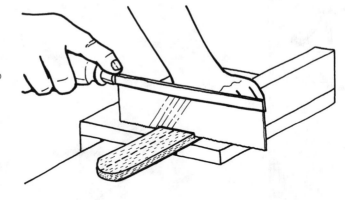

4-4 Use the tenon saw to establish the width and depth of the crossed half-lap channel.

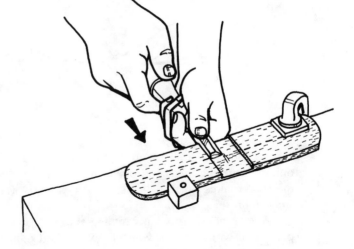

4-5 With one hand holding and guiding the chisel and the other hand pushing it, work with a careful paring action to remove the waste wood.

6. Having pared the crossed halving/half-lap channels to a good tight push-fit, set the two pieces of wood together for a trial fitting.

7. When you are happy with the fit, carefully ease the two pieces of wood apart and mark in the blade-twist areas that need to be lowered and wasted. The easiest method of marking the wood is to first set it down flat on the bench so that it is in north-south alignment, and then shade in the top right and the bottom left quarters. Do this with both lengths of wood, and on all sides (FIG. 4-6, left).

8. When you have established the areas that need to be cut away and wasted, take the wood a piece at a time, hold it in the north-south alignment so that it is pointing away from your body, and then use the knife to pare away the

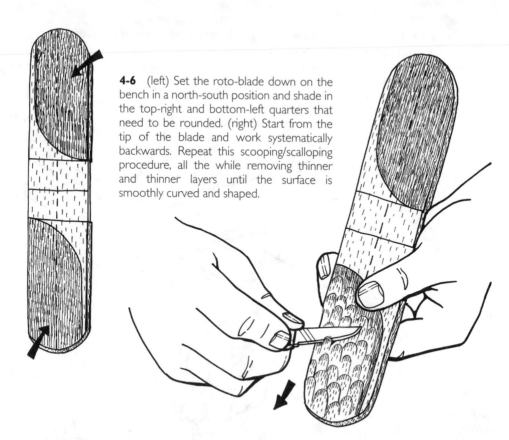

4-6 (left) Set the roto-blade down on the bench in a north-south position and shade in the top-right and bottom-left quarters that need to be rounded. (right) Start from the tip of the blade and work systematically backwards. Repeat this scooping/scalloping procedure, all the while removing thinner and thinner layers until the surface is smoothly curved and shaped.

shaded areas of waste. Work the rotoblade from center to end so that you are always cutting and slicing away from your body. Continue paring away at one end, turning the wood over, and doing the other end, and so on, until the wood takes on the characteristic prop-twist (FIG. 4-6, right). Sand to a smooth finish.

Note: A good tip when whittling is to sit down with your lap and knees protected, working with your elbows tucked tight into your waist, and cut only small slivers of waste away, working with a steady, controlled action.

9. When you have achieved the twist, smear a small amount of PVA glue on mating faces, and clamp the two lengths of wood together to make the crossed vane. When the glue is dry, remove the clamp, fix the spindle dowel center point by drawing diagonals across the square boss, and then drill the hole through with the ¼-inch-diameter bit.

Note: When you are drilling, always secure the workpiece with a clamp, and always have pieces of scrap wood between the workpiece and the bench, and the workpiece and the clamp.

10. Take the 7-inch length of 1-x-1-inch-square wood, and mark it off with all the step-off measurements that make up the design (FIG. 4-1). The finished handle needs to be 6 inches long, all bevels/chamfers are ¼ inch wide—on top,

sides and bottom—and the ½-inch-diameter pull-cord hole is centered ½ inch down from the top end.

11. Set the wood top-end-up in the vice and use the block plane to shave off the corners to make the chamfer. Work at a low, slanting angle to the corners to avoid splitting the wood. Repeat this procedure with both ends.

12. When you are ready to bore out the two holes—the ½-inch-diameter hole in the side for the pull-cord, and the ⅜-inch-diameter hole in the top for the spindle—reposition the handle top end-up in the vice, and back it with a piece of scrap wood to protect the wood as the ½-inch bit exits (FIG. 4-7).

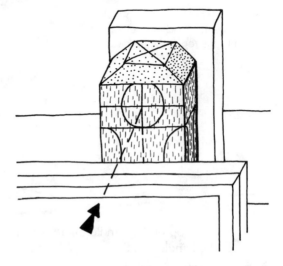

4-7 (left) Back the workpiece with some scrap wood, secure it top-end-up in the vice, and run it through with the ½-inch-diameter bit. Note—the scrap wood prevents the drill bit tearing the workpiece as it exits.

13. Fix the position of the spindle hole by drawing crossed diagonals. When you are happy with the arrangement, bore the ½-inch hole right through the 1-inch width, and then sink the ⅜-inch-diameter spindle hole ⅞ inch down into the top of the handle (FIG. 4-8).

14. Having noted how the side-of-handle corner chamfers start and finish ¾ inch along from the ends of the handle, set the handle flat-down in the vice, and then use the bevel-edge chisel to pare away the corners so as to create the chamfer (FIG. 4-9). Cut down to the ¼-inch-from-corner guidelines. Carefully and cautiously cut one curved end, turn the wood around in the vice to cut the other, and then clear the waste by paring from end-to-end. Continue working from end-to-center, and be very careful not to dig too deep or to let the chisel run out of control. Repeat until all four chamfers have been cut.

15. Rub down the ends of the 2-inch-long, ¼-inch-diameter spindle dowel to a smooth, rounded finish. Slide the spindle down into the top of the handle—it should be a loose, easy fit—pencil mark the position of the cord hole, and then ask a helper to hold the workpiece secure while you bore the hole through with the ⅛-inch drill bit. Glue-fix the spindle through the center of the crossed rotoblades, so that when the blades in the ready-to-launch posi-

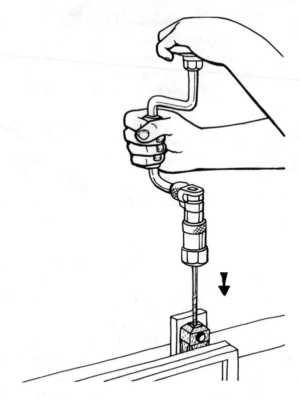

4-8 With the drill straight up-and-down, bore the ⅜-inch-diameter hole down into the top of the handle.

tion on top of the handle, there is a space of about ¼ inch between the top of the handle and the underside of the blades.

A couple of good tips: Cut a small groove along the length of the spindle to be glued. Also, when you are tapping the dowel through the crossed joint, support it over a scrap of wood that has been drilled with a larger hole (FIG. 4-10).

16. Rub the whole workpiece down to a smooth finish—all edges, ends, faces, and sides. Wipe away the dust, mask off the dowel spindle, and move to the area set aside for painting. Look again at the project picture (page 36), and note the areas of the rotoblades and the handle that we have painted red (the shaded areas on the grid).

    Use the acrylic paint and the fine-point brush to decorate the vanes accordingly. When the acrylic paint is completely dry, give the whole toy a couple of coats of varnish with a light sanding between coats.

17. When the varnish is dry, all systems are GO, and you can put on your flying goggles and have your first tryout. Knot the ring onto one end of the cord, and set the crossed rotoblades in place on top of the launch-pad handle. Pass one end of the cord through the spindle hole, and wind the blades in a clockwise direction so that the cord is wound onto the spindle. Then hold the handle at arm's length, check for all-clear, give a sharp tug on the pull-cord ring, and watch as the vane spins into motion. We have lift-off!

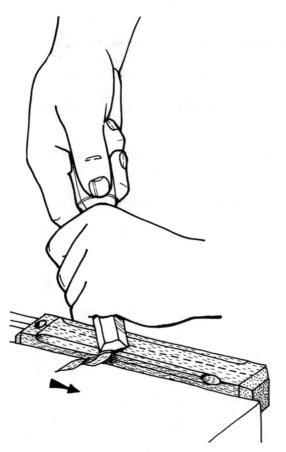

4-9 With the chisel held in both hands, take long, shallow, slicing cuts to achieve the chamfer.

4-10 Establish the pivot/dowel area that is to be glued through the rotoblades, cut a small groove and apply the glue. Set the rotoblades upside down over a piece of pre-drill waste wood and carefully tap the spindle down and through to the marker.

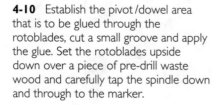

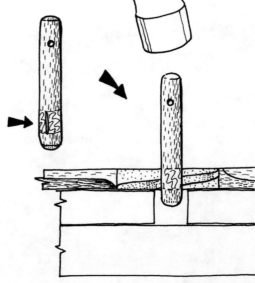

WATCHPOINTS

Because the rotoblades need to be simultaneously light in weight, strong, and made from an easy-to-carve wood, you need to choose your wood with extra care. If you can't find lime/linden or jelutong, ask your specialist supplier for advice.

If you have any doubts as to how the rotoblade twist is cut and carved, then have a pre-project tryout with some scrap wood.

If you don't much like the idea of using a knife to whittle the rotoblades to shape, you could clamp the wood to the bench and use a chisel.

If you think the handle design is a bit too fussy, you could make it from a length of broomstick dowel.

5
Walk tall

Making a pair of stilts:

A pair of traditional stilts with easy-to-move treads.

Primary techniques:

Using a coping saw, drilling and plugging, using a drawknife, sanding and painting.

Age level: 10–12

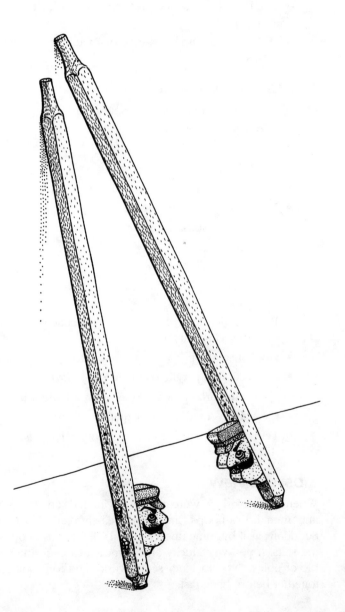

WOODS

Note: In the context of a pair of stilts, it is most important that your chosen wood is in good condition. If the 1½-x-1½-inch-square wood looks in any way to be split, warped, or knotty, then look around for a better piece. (The same goes for the footrests.)

- Two 60-inch lengths of prepared 1½-x-1½-inch-square section wood for the two poles. You need a strong, straight-grained, knot-free wood, such as beech or white pine.
- An 18-inch length of prepared 1½-x-4-inch section wood for the two footrests.
- A 10-inch length of ¾-inch-diameter broomstick dowel for the four bolts' plugs.

TOOLS AND MATERIALS

- Coping saw and a pack of spare blades
- Tenon saw
- Drawknife
- Bench with a vice
- One sheet each of workout and tracing paper
- Pencil, ruler, and try square
- A pair of compasses/dividers
- Marking gauge
- One pack of two-tube resin glue
- Power drill and stand, or bench/press drill, with drill bits at ¼-inch, ⅜-inch, and ¾-inch diameter
- Four 4½-inch long, ¼-inch-diameter coach bolts with four washers and four butterfly wing nuts to fit
- Graded sandpaper
- A selection of acrylic paints in *pink, dark blue, black, white,* and *red*
- Two soft-haired paintbrushes, a broad and a fine-point
- Clear, high-shine, exterior-quality varnish
- Two rubber chair-leg caps at about 1 inch diameter to fit the bottom of the stilt poles

KIDS'-EYE VIEW

When I was a kid we were always having fads and rages for toys. First it was yo-yos, and then hoola-hoops, and then pea-shooters. Then one summer, it was stilts. Suddenly, as if by some unseen signal, all the kids in our street were frantically making stilts. If you were lucky and owned a tool kit, then it was no problem—a couple of poles, two blocks of scrap wood, and four bolts, and the stilts could be put together before breakfast.

Although my stilts were not so beautiful—more splits and splinters than anything else—the feeling of walking tall was really fantastic. It was like being older and more important . . . like being another person.

The stilts in this project are extra fun because the treads look like a couple of heads—a sea captain or general, you can take your pick.

Just imagine, not only will you be taller, but—better still—you will be walking along the street with your feet resting on a pair of heads—ha!

CAREGIVERS' GUIDE

Making Time and Skill Level—No real problems with this project, if the child knows how to use a coping saw, a drawknife, and drill, then it's all pretty straightforward.

That said, because the spacing of the holes is critical, you really need to use a power drill in a stand or a bench press drill. If you are around to help with the drawknife and the hole spacing, and the child is keen, then I would say that an average 10- to 12-year-old will have the stilts made in the space of a long weekend.

Cautions and Adult Help—At first sight, the drawknife looks to be a dangerous and difficult-to-use tool. However, in use with the knife being held in both hands and drawn towards the user it's almost impossible for the user to do damage to him-/herself.

Having said that, and bearing in mind that the drawknife does need to be sharp, then you will, of course, need to be helping, or at the very least close by and watching over the child. Like most woodworking procedures, though, if the wood is held secure and the tool is sharp, and if the child is working at the correct height, then it's just about as safe as it can be.

It is necessary to bore lots of accurate holes, so it's much easier to use a power drill in a stand—or, better still, a bench press drill—rather than hand-held drill.

Be Warned—For safety's sake, if two or more children are working on the same project, then there needs to be plenty of room for the children to be able to move around freely without tripping over each other.

GETTING DOWN TO WORK

1. Have a look at the project picture (page 47), the working drawing (FIG. 5-1), and the design template (FIG. 5-2), and see how the stilts are made from four wooden parts—two poles and two footrests. Note the way the comical footrests are held in place by captive coach bolts and wing nuts. The bolts are set 4 inches apart, and the poles are drilled at 1-inch intervals so the footrests can be raised or lowered by 1-inch steps.

2. On the 18-inch length of prepared 4-x-1½-inch section wood—the piece for the two footrests—measure 9 inches along from one end, and then cut the piece into two with the tenon saw.

3. Label the various faces of the wood top-of-hat, FRONT, SIDE, and BACK. Do this with both pieces.

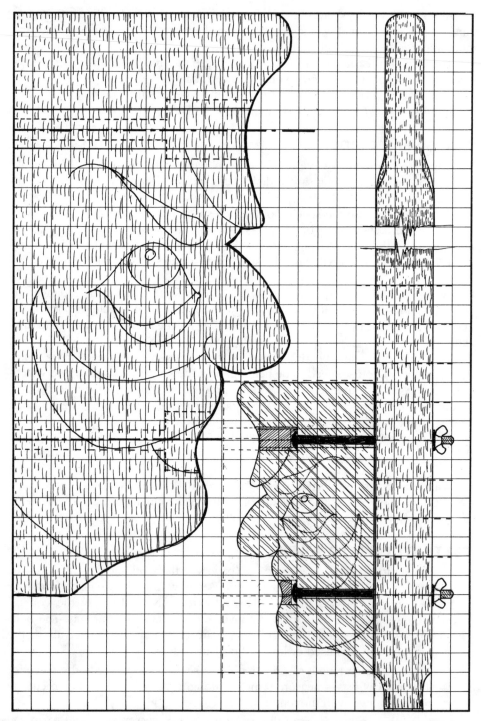

5-1 Working Drawing. (left) The scale of the footrest is 4 grid squares to 1 inch. (right) The scale is 2 grid squares to 1 inch.

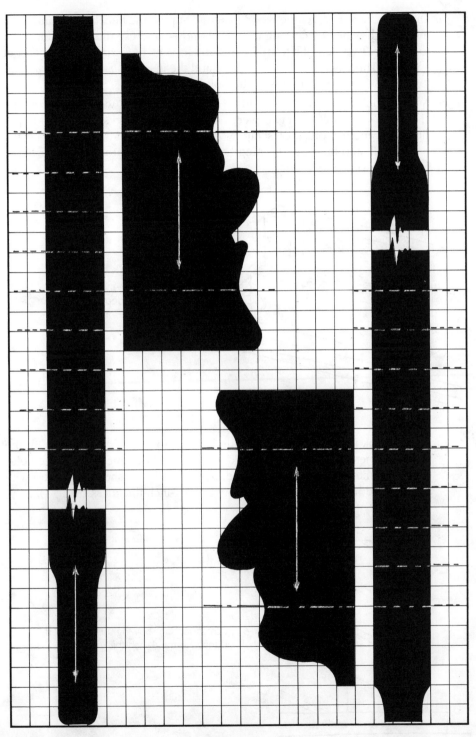

5-2 Design Template. The scale is 2 grid squares to 1 inch.

4. One piece at a time, set the wood front-face-up on the bench—meaning with the 1½-inch-wide, 9-inch-long face uppermost—and use the pencil and ruler to measure two step-offs from the top end, one at 1½ inches and the other at 4 inches. This done, use the try square and the marking gauge (set at ¾ inch) to establish the center points of the bolt holes.

5. Ask an adult to help with the drill. Now, still with the wood front-face-up, clamp the wood between two pieces of scrap wood, and secure them in position on another piece of scrap wood. Fit the ¾-inch-diameter bit in the bench drill, and bore out the plug holes—two on each footrest—to a depth of 2 inches (FIG. 5-3).

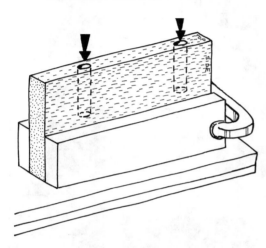

5-3 Drill the ¾-inch-diameter plug holes out to a depth of 2 inches.

6. Having sunk the ¾-inch-diameter plug holes in to a depth of 2 inches, fit the ¼-inch-diameter bit in the drill chuck, and run the bottom-centers of the holes the rest of the way through the wood. If all is well, you should finish up with a step-sided hole that runs right through the 4-inch thickness (FIG. 5-4).

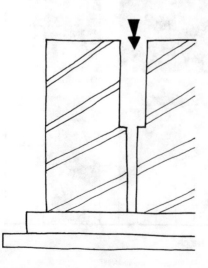

5-4 A cross section showing the step-sided holes that run through the 4-inch thickness.

7. One at a time, take the ¼-inch coach bolts, slide them down into their holes, and screw them tight with the washers and wing nuts. Tighten up on the nut until the bolt head is at the bottom of the plug hole, and the square shank underneath the bolt head has been drawn down into the ¼-inch hole to be a tight wedge fit (FIG. 5-5).

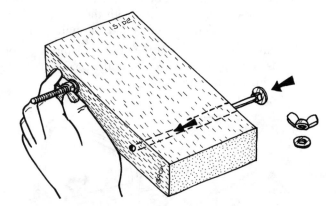

5-5 Tighten up the nut to draw the square shank bolt head into the ¼-inch-diameter hole to make a tight-wedge fit.

8. Using a tenon saw to cut a small air/glue vent/slot along the 10-inch length of ¾-inch-wide broomstick dowel, secure in the vice with a clamped saw-guide strip (FIG. 5-6). Saw the dowel into four 2½-inch-long plugs and trim the plugs to size so that they are a tight push-fit in the bolt holes.

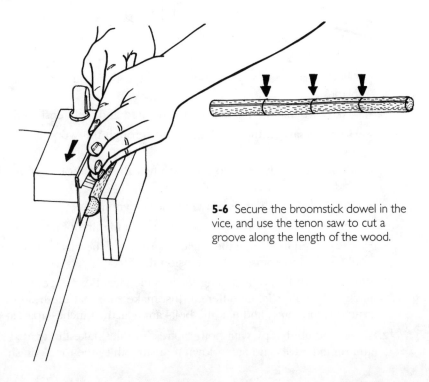

5-6 Secure the broomstick dowel in the vice, and use the tenon saw to cut a groove along the length of the wood.

9. Now, with the footrest blocks clamped tight in the jaws of the vice so that the wide plugs' holes are uppermost, generously smear the plugs with two-tube resin glue and tap them home into the holes. While the glue is drying, draw the footrest "head profile" design up to full size, (FIG. 5-1) and make a clear tracing.

10. Set the tracing down on the side face of the footrest block so that the straight top-of-cap line is aligned with the top end, and then use a hard pencil to press-transfer the traced outline through to the wood. Do this on both blocks.

11. Having set out the profile design, clamp the wood securely in the vice, and use the coping saw to cut out the profile (FIG. 5-7). The rules of thumb when using a coping saw are:

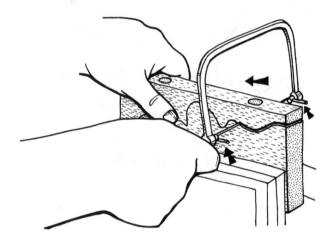

5-7 With the footrest secured in the vice, use the coping saw to cut out the head-shaped profile.

- Check that the tool is in good order and that you have a pack of spare blades.
- Make sure that the blade is correctly fitted and well tensioned.
- Hold the saw so that the blade runs through the wood at right angles to the face of the wood.
- Work at a steady pace so as not to tear the wood or twist and break the blade.
- Work a little to the waste side of the drawn line.
- Keep the blade of the saw presented with the line of next cut.
- If you need to change the angle/approach of the blade, unscrew the handle, swivel the pins, and pretension the blade.

Although you should be aiming for two identical heads, it doesn't matter too much if they are slightly different. Just make sure that the head-height-from-ground is the same, and that the bolts are exactly 4 inches apart at centers.

12. When you are happy with both footrest profiles, take the graded sandpaper and rub all edges and faces down to a smooth-to-the-touch finish.

13. Take the two 60-inch lengths of prepared 1½-x-1½-inch-square section wood—the wood for the poles—and label the ends TOP and BOTTOM, and one of the faces FOOTREST SIDE. With the pencil, ruler and try square, mark the wood off 1 inch along from the BOTTOM, and 4½ inches along from the TOP (FIG. 5-8).

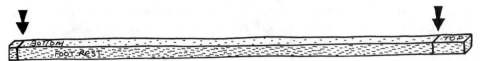

5-8 Mark the poles 1 inch along from the BOTTOM and 4½ inches along from the TOP.

14. Fix the end center points by drawing crossed diagonals, then set the compass/dividers to a radius of ½ inch and scribe the ends of the wood off with 1-inch-diameter circles (FIG. 5-9, left). Set one of the poles in the vice so that it is at a low looking-at-your-belt angle, and so that you can approach it TOP end on. Take the drawknife in both hands and gently shave away the corners of the wood until the top 4½-inch length is more or less round and 1-inch diameter in section (FIG. 5-9, right). Repeat this procedure with both ends of both poles, and then use the sandpaper to rub the rounded ends down to a smooth pleasant-to-hold finish.

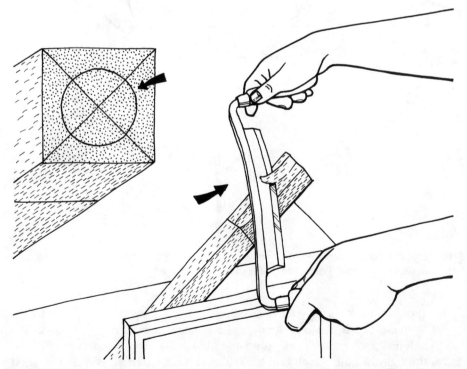

5-9 (left) Find the center point by drawing crossed diagonals and scribe a 1-inch-diameter circle. (right) Use a drawknife to shave and shape the end.

15. When you have rounded off the ends, position the poles on the workbench so that the FOOTREST face is uppermost. Set the marking gauge to ¾ inch, and run a centerline mark from TOP to BOTTOM along the length of the wood.

16. Clamp the poles side-by-side on the bench. Using a pencil, ruler, and try square and starting 3 inches along from BOTTOM and working towards the TOP, set the centerlines off with 16 carefully measured 1-inch step-offs. Use the try square to run the step-offs across both lengths of wood (FIG. 5-10, top).

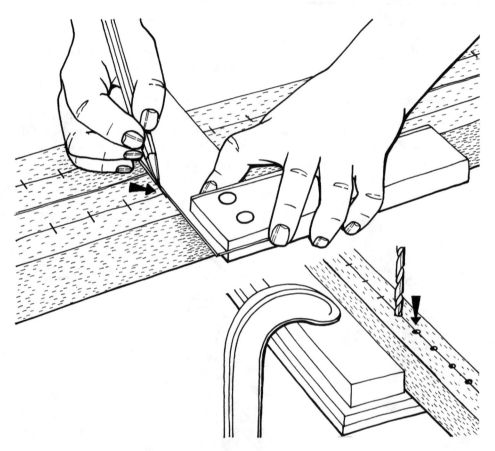

5-10 (top) Mark the 1-inch step-offs and use the try square to run the measurements across both pole widths. (bottom) Bore out the line of ⅜-inch-diameter holes.

17. Have an adult check your measurements and set up the drill press for you. With the 1-inch step-offs clearly and accurately marked on both poles, clamp a fence and waste wood onto the drill-press table, and bore the holes through with the ⅜-inch drill bit. (FIG. 5-10, bottom). If all is well, you should be able to select any one of the height settings and bolt the footrest(s) in place.

18. When you are happy with the poles—the handles, the spacing and fit of the holes, and the footrests—take the graded sandpaper and rub all the surfaces down to a smooth slightly round-edged finish.

19. Having wiped away the dust, move to the area set aside for painting, and make a tracing of the footrest design using the painting grid (FIG. 5-11).

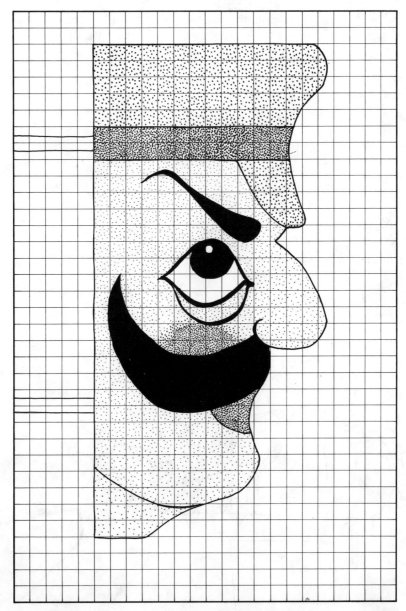

5-11 Painting grid. The scale is 4 grid squares to 1 inch. The face is pink; the hat is blue; the hatband, lips, and cheeks are red; the eyes are white; and the hair and detail lines are black.

Next support the footrests on some scrap wood. The working order is:

- Give the footrests an all-over coat of pink acrylic paint.
- Let the paint dry and give it a swift rubdown with a fine grade sandpaper.
- Pencil-press transfer the line of the cap design through to both sides of the footrests (FIG. 5-12).
- Paint the caps dark blue, and the eyes white.
- Use the fine-point brush, to paint the eye and whisker details black and the cap bands, cheeks and lips red, and leave to dry (FIG. 5-13).

20. Finally, lightly sand down between coats, give all surfaces a couple of coats of varnish, and let the varnish dry. Then fit the anti-skid chair-leg caps, and the stilts are ready for walking!

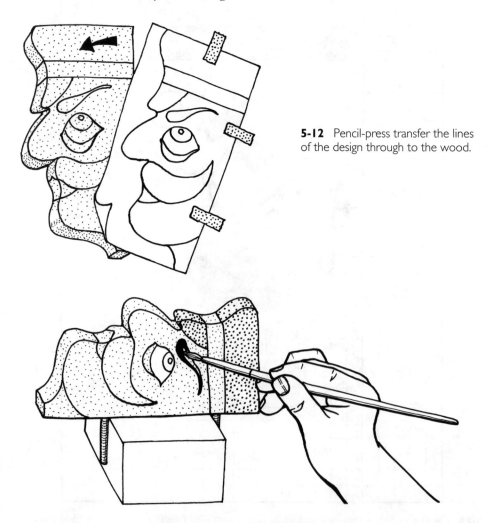

5-12 Pencil-press transfer the lines of the design through to the wood.

5-13 Use the fine-point brush to paint in the design details.

WATCHPOINTS

If you like the idea of making stilts but are worried about the use of a drawknife, you could modify the forms and shape the poles with a surform type rasp.

If you can get to use a large 12-inch-blade electric scroll saw, then you could sandwich the two footrest pieces together with strips of double-sided sticky tape and cut the two head profiles out at one and the same time. Working in this way it is possible to achieve two identical profiles.

You could glue strips of anti-skid rubber on top of the footrests.

If you like the idea of the project, but are not so keen on having head-shaped brackets to stand on, then you could go for plain brackets, or have just about any shape that takes your fancy.

If you can't get to use a power drill, bearing in mind that the holes do need to be accurately placed, you could either make-do with fewer holes, or use a hand drill, and take a lot of care.

6
Bird call

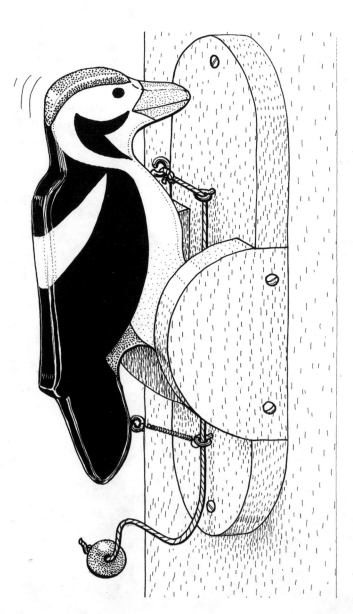

Making a woodpecker door knocker:

A pivoted and sprung pull-and-tap door knocker.

Primary techniques:

Compass work, fretting, shaping, half-lap jointing, drilling, using dowels, gluing, screwing, and painting.

Age level: 10–11

WOODS

- A length of prepared ½-inch-thick wood at 20 inches long and 2½ inches wide for the backboard and sideplates. It's best to use a straight-grained wood like beech, white pine, or jelutong.
- A length of prepared 1-inch-thick easy-to-carve wood at 8 inches long and 4½ inches wide for the woodpecker. Ideally, you need a knot-free, smooth-grained wood like lime/linden, or cherry.
- A 2-inch length of ¼-inch-diameter dowel.

TOOLS AND MATERIALS

- Coping saw and a pack of spare blades
- Bench with a vice
- Bench hook
- Workout and tracing paper
- Pencil and ruler
- Try square
- A pair of compasses or dividers
- Small hand drill with a selection of bits to fit
- Four ¾-inch-long roundhead brass screws
- One ¾-inch-long tension spring
- Four brass screw-eyes
- One slender ½-inch-long brass brad or pin
- One 12-inch length of cord (It needs to be able to pass through the screw-eyes)
- White PVA glue
- One large painted wooden bead
- Bradawl
- Screwdriver to fit the screws
- Graded sandpaper
- Small surform open-toothed tube rasp
- Acrylic paints in the colors *red, white, yellow,* and *black.*
- Two paintbrushes: a broad and a fine-point
- Clear, high-gloss varnish
- A couple of roundhead brass screws to fix the knocker to the door

KIDS'-EYE VIEW

You are sitting quietly in your bedroom, and trying really hard to concentrate on your homework. Suddenly the door bursts open, and without so much as a "please" or "thank you," your kid brother or dad or mom charges in, finds what it is they are looking for, and then charges out again. And there you are, left high and dry, with your line of thought broken.

Enough is enough! It's about time you fitted a knocker to your door and educated the family. The highly civilized idea is, they should quietly tap on the door, and you should just as quietly give them the OK. As to whether the marauders (meaning noisy looters) will bother to knock . . . well, I think that the woodpecker is so funny, they won't be able to resist it. The next question you have to ask yourself is, will your kid brother or sister be able to settle for one, two, or maybe three knocks, or are they just going to keep on tap, tap, tapping?

CAREGIVERS' GUIDE

Making Time and Skill Level—No real problems with this project, as long as the child knows how to use a coping saw.

Although the final stage—fixing the spring and the string—is somewhat finger-twisting, an average 10- to 11-year-old should be able to build this project in about 8–10 hours.

Cautions and Adult Help—Fitting a number of components together to make a smooth-working whole is always a little bit tricky. And so it is with this project—the spring has to be just right, the pivot mustn't be too tight, too loose, or crooked, the string mustn't be too fat or too hairy, and so on. The whole thing needs to be thought out.

With a project of this character, it's best if there is an adult on standby, ready to give a helping hand, especially at the putting-together stage.

GETTING DOWN TO WORK

1. Have a look at the project picture (page 60), the working drawings (FIG. 6-1), and the template picture (FIG. 6-2), and see how the woodpecker door knocker is made up from 12 primary components—a backboard, two half-circle sideplates, the woodpecker, a short length of dowel, four screw-eyes, a tension or pull spring, a length of cord, and a large wooden bead—all put together with glue and screws. Note the direction of the grain, and the way the two sideplates are notched or half-lapped into the backboard so that they are set parallel to each other, and at right angles.

2. Check that the wood is in good condition, draw the design up to full size, and make careful tracings.

3. Pencil-press transfer the traced designs through to the wood. Have the backboard and the two sideplates on the ½-inch-thick board, and the woodpecker on the 1-inch-thick easy-to-carve wood (FIG. 6-3).

4. Use a pencil, ruler, try squares, and compasses to establish and rework the curves, the centerlines, and the position of all the holes. If it helps, label the components and shade in areas that need to be cut away.

5. When you have fixed the position and diameter of all the holes, clamp the wood down securely, or ask a friend to help while you run the holes through

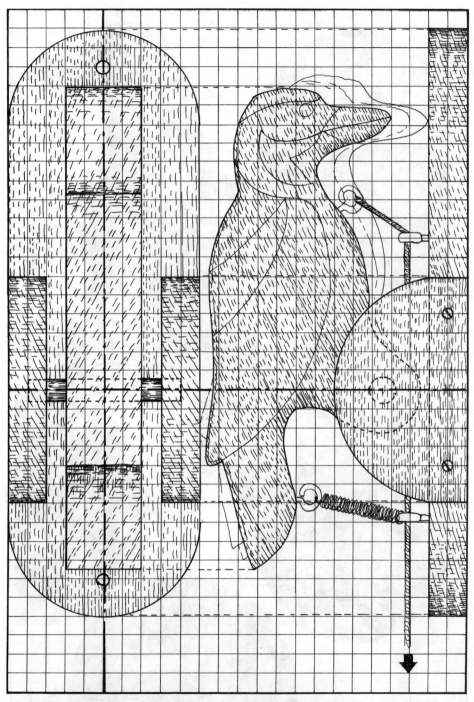

6-1 Working Drawing. At a scale of 4 grid squares to 1 inch, the doorplate is 7¾ inches long and 2½ inches wide, while the total depth from the back of the woodpecker through to the door is about 3½ inches. Note the position of the screw-eyes and the main pivot.

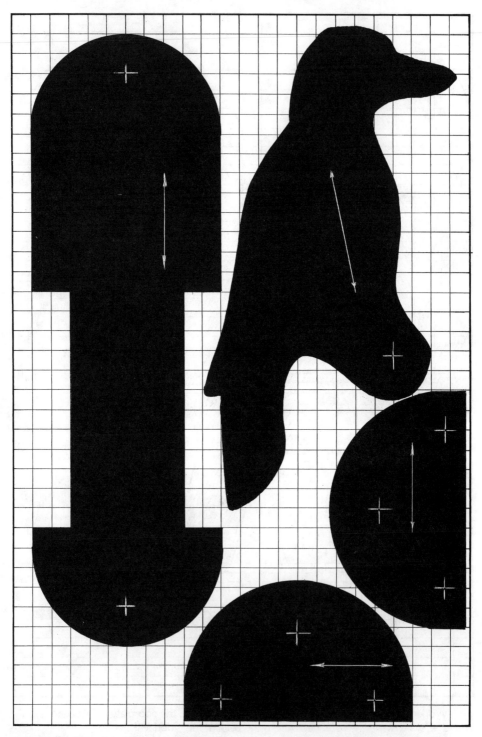

6-2 Design Template. The scale is 4 grid squares to 1 inch. Note the direction of the grain.

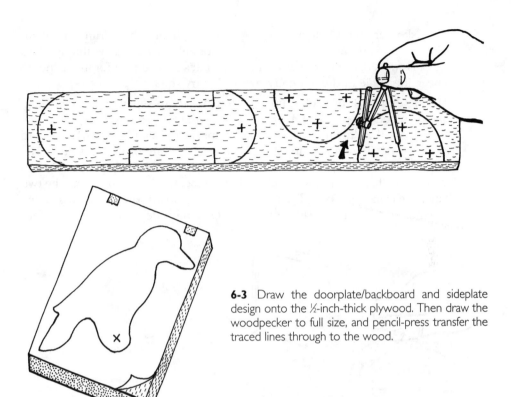

6-3 Draw the doorplate/backboard and sideplate design onto the ½-inch-thick plywood. Then draw the woodpecker to full size, and pencil-press transfer the traced lines through to the wood.

with the hand drill and the appropriate size bits. Use the ³⁄₁₆-inch-diameter bit for the two hanging holes on the top and bottom of the backplate, the ⅛-inch-diameter bit for the screw-fixing sideplates' holes, the ¼-inch-diameter bit for the through-bird hole, and the ⁵⁄₁₆-inch-diameter bit for the sideplate dowel holes. Because the sideplate dowel holes need to be *blind* (meaning they don't go right through the wood, but rather they are only sunk to a depth of ¼ inch), wrap a tape depth guide around the drill bit (FIG. 6-4).

6-4 After wrapping the drill bit in masking tape, drill ¼-inch-deep blind holes—one on each sideplate.

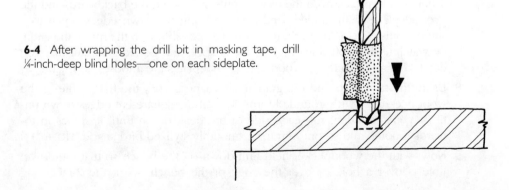

Ask your friend/helper to align the drill so that the holes run at right angles to the working face. This is very important because if the through-bird pivot is twisted, the woodpecker might jam. It's a good idea for the helper to check the angle of drill bit entry/exit with a try square.

6. Having drilled all the holes, use the straight saw to separate the units, then set the wood a piece at a time in the jaws of the vice and use the coping saw to fret out the drawn shapes. The woodpecker is simple because the bird profile is flexible enough to allow for a small amount of blade wander. The backboard and sideplates, on the other hand, need to be precisely cut and worked so that they fit together. The best procedure is to first cut out the two sideplates and the overall shape of the backboard, and then to cut the notched half-laps to fit (FIG. 6-5). Aim to have the sideplates a tight push-fit.

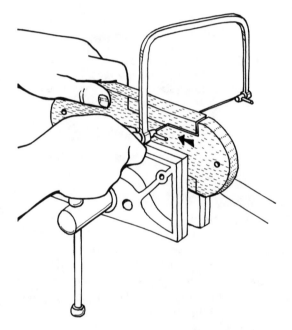

6-5 Cut the notched laps to make a tight push-fit for the sideplates.

7. When you have achieved the four cutouts, rub down the backboard, and the two sideplates with graded sandpaper to bring the sawn edges down to a smooth finish (FIG. 6-6). Working as much as possible with the run of the grain, be watchful that you don't blur all the shapes, and be extra careful that you don't sand away so much wood that the sideplates are a loose, sloppy fit.

8. Using the tube rasp and the graded sandpaper, work the flat profile of the woodpecker to partly rounded form. Rub all the square-cut edges down until they are rounded, rub each side of the beak down until it angles in towards a point, and so on. Aim for a smoothly stylized bird shape (FIG. 6-7).

9. Now, with the woodpecker held firm-down on the bench so that the dowel hole is over a hole or over the edge of the bench, mark the 2-inch-long

6-6 Working in the direction of the grain, rub the cut notches down to a good fit and finish.

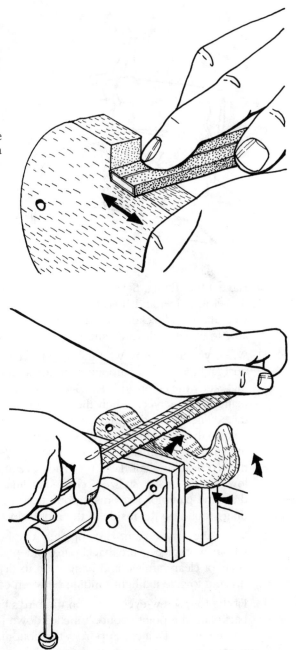

6-7 Use the tube rasp to rub the square-cut edges down to a smooth-rounded profile.

dowel at ½ inch in from each end, and tap it through the hole so that ½ inch sticks out at either side of the bird (FIG. 6-8). When you are happy with the fit, fix the dowel in place by tapping the brass pin/brad into the underside edge of the bird and on through into the dowel.

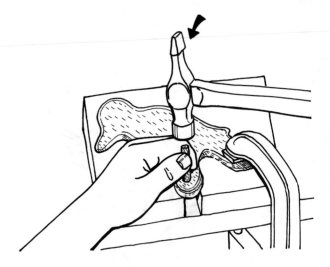

6-8 Tap the dowel through the pivot hole so that ½ inch sticks out at either side of the bird.

10. Have a trial fitting. Set one sideplate in its slot, slide the woodpecker pivot dowel in place, and hold the bird in position with the other plate. If all is well, the woodpecker should be nicely contained and yet free enough to be able to move backwards and forwards on its pivot.

11. When you are happy with the way the project fits together, wipe away the dust and move the components to the area that has been set aside for painting. Study the color grid (FIG. 6-9). Start by giving the bird an all-over coat of matte white acrylic. When the white paint is dry, pencil-press transfer the traced lines of the design through to both sides of the bird, and then carefully link up the side-of-bird designs by running the lines around the edges. Take the small-point brush and paint in all the details that make up the design—the red head and tail flash, the black eye and feather markings, and the yellow beak. Aim for stylized, clean-line imagery. From shape to shape, first draw the paint-loaded brush around the pencil line so that the brush hairs drag around on the inside of the motif/block, and then fill in the shape.

12. When the acrylic paint is completely dry, set up a drying line and give the whole workpiece—the backboard, sideplates, and the bird—a couple of coats of clear varnish, and hang it up to dry. Don't forget to let the varnish dry and to give it a light sanding between coats.

13. Fit the four screw-eyes—one on the bird's breast, one on its tail, one on the backplate at a point about 2¾ inches down from the top, and another one at a point about 1¼ inches up from the bottom. You might need to use the pliers to open the screw-eyes so that you can slide the ends of the spring into place. *Be warned:* If you try to bend and shape the spring, it might snap. You might need to make starter holes with the bradawl. Have all the screw-eyes set on the centerline, and aligned so that there is a smooth and easy passage for the pull-cord (FIG. 6-10, top).

14. Glue and screw one sideplate into position, locate one end of the through-

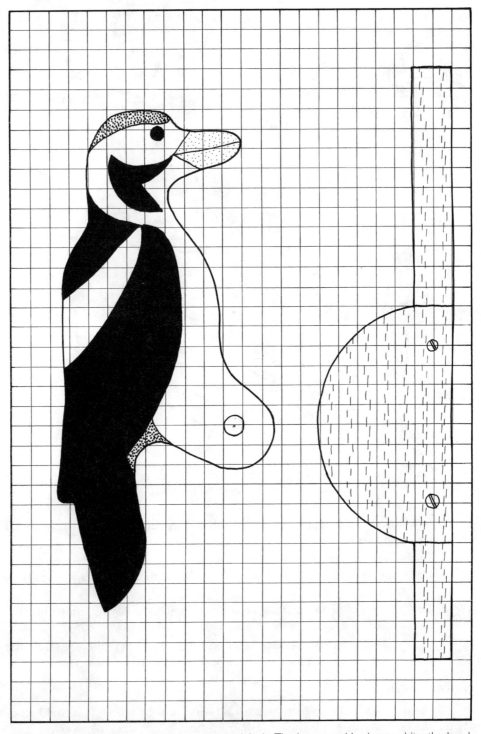

6-9 Color grid. The scale is 4 grid squares to 1 inch. The breast and back are white, the head-cap and under-tail are red, the beak is yellow, the tail and wings are black, and the doorplate is left the natural color of the wood.

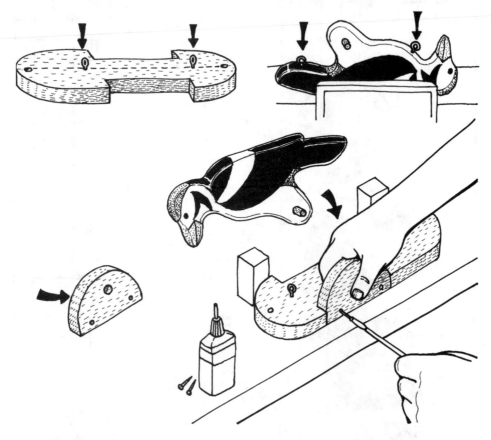

6-10 (top left) Fit the screw-eyes to the doorplate, and then to the bird. (bottom) Fit the bird/pivot in the blind hole, and then screw the other sideplate in place.

bird dowel in the plate hole, set the other sideplate in position, and fix with glue and two screws (FIG. 6-10, bottom).

15. Fit the tension spring between the bottom two screw-eyes—the one on the bird's tail and the one 1¼ inches up from the bottom of the backboard (FIG. 6-11, top).

16. Knot the pull cord on the bird's breast, and then run it down through the two backboard screw-eyes (FIG. 6-11, bottom).

17. Finally, knot the large wooden bead on the end of the pull-cord, screw the knocker on the door, and stand back and wait for the action!

WATCHPOINTS

If you like the idea of the project but are a bit short of solid wood, you could modify the design and make the whole knocker up from ½-inch-thick plywood.

If you have trouble obtaining the tension or pull spring, you could use a heavy-duty elastic band.

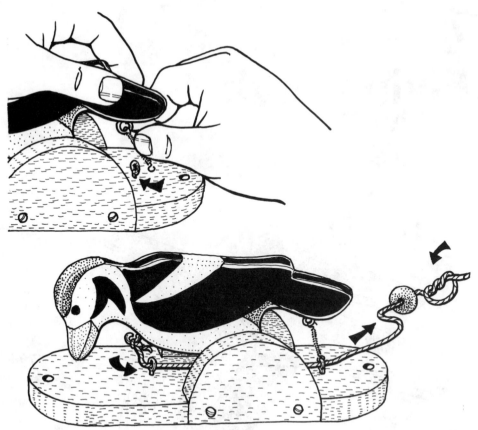

6-11 (top) Fit the tension spring between the bottom two tail-end screw-eyes. (bottom) Knot the pull-cord on the bird's breast, thread it down through the two doorplate screw-eyes, and knot on the bead.

7
Flying high

Making a wooden airplane:

A high-wing plane with wheels and a whizz-around propeller.

Primary techniques:

Sawing, fretting, cutting half-lap joints, slot joints, drilling, whittling and painting.

Age level:

11–12

WOODS

- A 6-inch length of prepared wood at 1¼ inches wide and ½ inch thick for the fuselage and legs. Best to go for a straight-grained knot-free wood like beech or white pine.
- A sheet of best-quality birch-faced ⅛-inch-thick multicore plywood at about 6 × 6 inches for the wings and wheels.
- A 3-inch length of prepared wood at about ½-x-½-inch-square section, for the propeller. You need to use an easy-to-carve wood like lime/linden or sycamore.

TOOLS AND MATERIALS

- Fretsaw and a pack of spare blades
- Bird's mouth fretsaw board with a bench clamp
- Small tenon or gents saw
- Small bench clamp
- Workbench with a vice
- Workout and tracing paper
- Pencil, ruler, and try square.
- A pair of compasses
- Small penknife for whittling
- Bradawl
- Hand drill and selection of bits to fit
- Five brass roundhead screws—4 at ½ inch long and 1 at 1 inch.
- Eight brass washers to fit the screws
- White PVA wood glue
- Screwdriver to fit the screws
- Graded sandpaper
- Red acrylic paint
- Two brushes: a broad and a fine-point
- High-shine varnish.

KIDS'-EYE VIEW

Slowly spinning and failing, turning and drifting across a sun-flashed flickering of blue-white skies . . . Just imagine: you pull back on the control column and—whooosh!—the plane comes out of its dive and levels off. The sky is a brilliant, clear blue, the clouds are like fluffy scoops of ice cream—and there you are, in control of the airplane.

Okay, so you are only a kid, and you have never flown in a real plane, but not to worry, because now is the time to make your very own high-wing, single-prop airplane toy and to let your imagination carry you up into the great blue yonder.

This plane is a beauty. The propeller really does flip around in the wind. It's good fun.

CAREGIVERS' GUIDE

Making Time and Skill Level—Although the individual making stages aren't especially difficult, I think it's fair to say that this project is best suited to a child who enjoys lots of careful measuring and painstaking cutting. For example, see how the back wings and the tail slot into each other, and how the legs notch into the underside of the fuselage.

A keen 11- to 12-year-old (a well-motivated child who likes the notion of airplanes) should be able to have this plane made in a weekend.

Cautions and Adult Help—The child will almost certainly need help when it comes to making the propeller. Its not that the propeller is difficult to make, but rather it is more the case that it is difficult to visualize. Bearing in mind that the propeller involves a certain amount of controlled knife work, you have two options. You can stay close at hand while the child is cutting the wood, or you can opt for buying an inexpensive ready-made plastic propeller.

Be Warned—In the context of whittling, a difficult-to-hold blunt knife is more dangerous than a comfortable-to-hold sharp one.

GETTING DOWN TO WORK

1. Have a look at the project picture (page 72), the working drawing (FIG. 7-1) and the design template (FIG. 7-2), and see how the plane is made up from nine component parts—a fuselage, a main wing, a tail wing, a tail/rudder, two wheels, and a propeller. See how, at a scale of 4 grid squares to 1 inch, the plane measures about 5 inches long from nose to tail, and 5 inches across the span of the wings. Note the slot-fitting of the legs into the underside of the plane, the slotted half-lap fitting of the small wing and tail into the fuselage, and the direct screw fitting of the main wing to the top of the fuselage.

2. Set the wood out on the workbench—the ply and the pine/ beech—and make sure that it's in good condition and free from such difficult-to-work faults as delaminations, splits, and hard or loose knots.

3. Draw the design up to full size, make tracings, and pencil-press transfer the traced designs through to the appropriate pieces of wood (FIG. 7-3). Set the compass to a radius of ⅝ inch and draw the two 1¼-inch-diameter wheels.

4. Having drawn in centerlines on the wings, mark the drawn out components so that you are clear in your own mind as to what goes where and how (the wheel center and the wing-fixing holes).

5. Clamp the bird's-mouth cutting board to the bench, and use the fretsaw to cut out all the plywood components—the wings, tail, and wheels (FIG. 7-4, left). The easiest way of working is to first separate each component from the large sheet, then cut around the drawn shapes in a counterclockwise direction, and

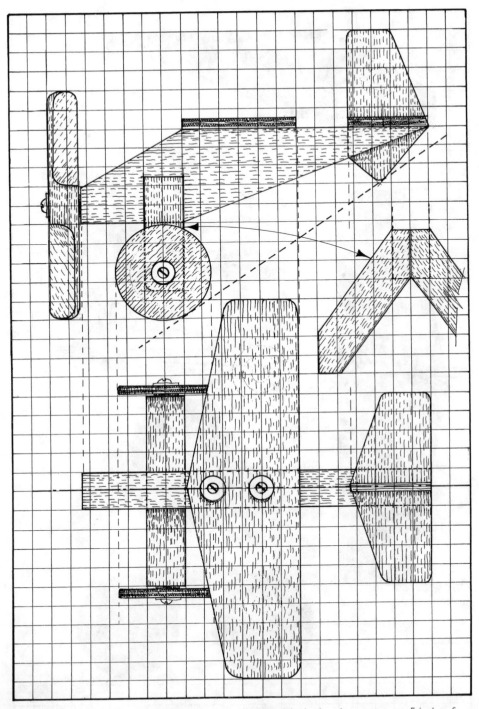

7-1 Working Drawing—At a scale of 4 grid squares to 1 inch, the plane measures 5 inches from nose to tail, and 5 inches wide across the span of the wings. Note how the legs splay out at an angle and are notched into the fuselage.

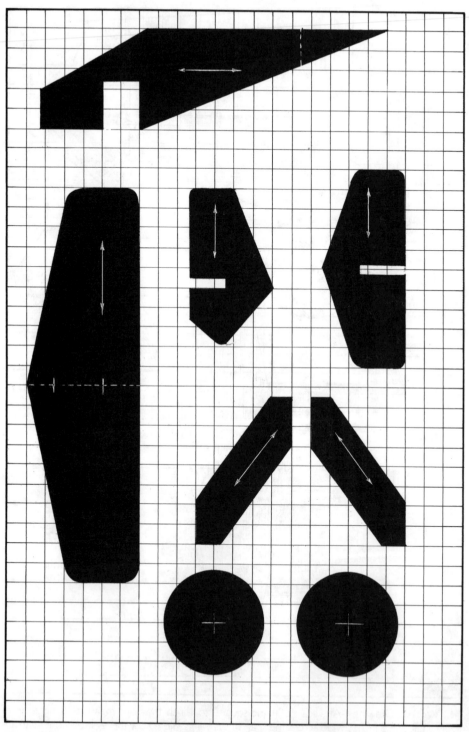

7-2 Design Templates—The scale is four grid squares to 1 inch.

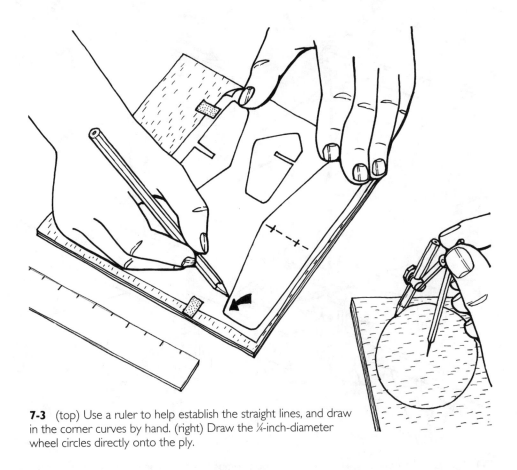

7-3 (top) Use a ruler to help establish the straight lines, and draw in the corner curves by hand. (right) Draw the ¼-inch-diameter wheel circles directly onto the ply.

finally cut the slots in two movements (FIG. 7-4, top right). Work at a slow, easy pace, all the while maneuvering both the wood and the saw so that the saw is presented with the next line of cut, and so that the cutline is a little to the waste side of the drawn line. Be careful not to force the pace and so rip the wood. To minimize wood-shake, try all the while to cut as near as possible to the vertex of the bird's-mouth V.

6. When you have achieved all the plywood cutouts, use the graded sandpaper to rub the faces and edges down to a smooth-to-the-touch finish. Try to keep the wheels circular by sanding the edges with a stroking action while at the same time turning the wheel. Aim for a good back wing to tail fit, and generally be careful not to blur the shape of the profiles and not to distort the joint slots.

7. Take the ½-inch-thick wood, check that the three components are nicely set out—the two legs and the fuselage—and then cut them out with the tenon saw. The two angled legs are straightforward: just a few straight cuts for each leg and the job is done (FIG. 7-5). The fuselage is slightly more tricky, but only

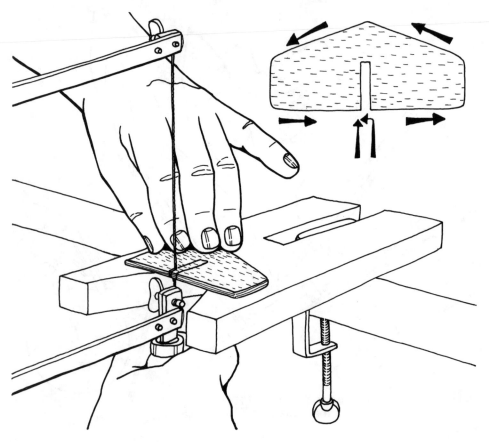

7-4 (left) Use the fretsaw to cut out the plywood components. (top right) Cut each profile in a counterclockwise direction.

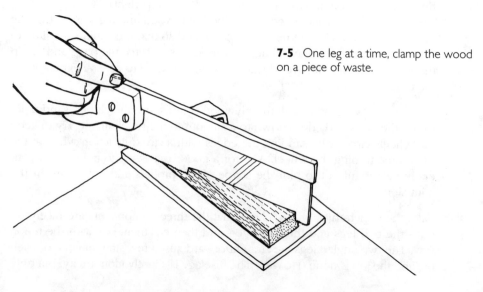

7-5 One leg at a time, clamp the wood on a piece of waste.

because the shape comes to a sharp angle at the tail. A good tip is to cut the long tail angle first (FIG. 7-6), then the cabin front, and finally the nose. Don't try at this stage to cut out the underbelly leg notch; just settle for cutting out the overall profile.

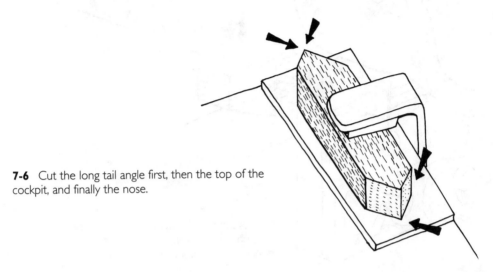

7-6 Cut the long tail angle first, then the top of the cockpit, and finally the nose.

8. When you have cut out the basic fuselage profile, take the pencil, measure, and try square and carefully mark in the position of the leg notch and the tail slot. Bear in mind that the legs and the tail need to be a tight push-fit.

9. With the fuselage well secured in the vice, take the tenon saw and—one joint at a time—establish the width and depth of the leg notch and the wing slot by making side-by-side parallel cuts (FIG. 7-7). Having cut to the waste sides of the drawn lines, take the fretsaw and link the bottom of the cuts so that the waste falls away (FIG. 7-8). Be careful about the fragile short grain between the top of the leg-notch and the cockpit nose. If need be, sand the joint for a good fit.

10. When you have established the position of the wheels on the leg ends by drawing crossed diagonals, spike the center point with the bradawl to make screw pilot holes. When you are ready to put the plane together, glue the splayed legs together and into the under-fuselage notch. Then glue and fit the back wings into the tail slot, and glue and screw the main wing to the top of the fuselage. Have brass washers between the head of the screw and the wood, and make sure that all centerlines are carefully aligned.

11. Take the 3-inch length of ½-x-½-inch-square wood—the piece for the propeller—fix the center point by drawing crossed diagonals, and draw in centerlines. When you have established the center point, take the drill and bore out a loose-fit hole for the pivot screw (FIG. 7-9).

12. Hold the propeller in your left hand so that the area to be worked is pointing towards you. Using the knife, make a series of small, thumb-supported

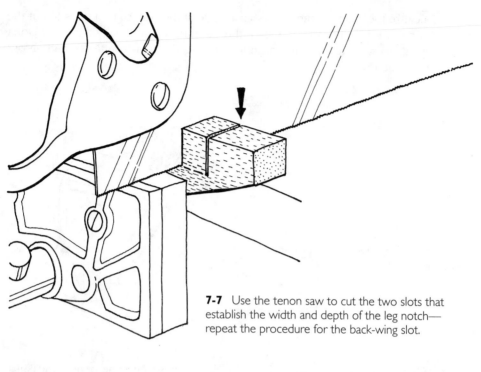

7-7 Use the tenon saw to cut the two slots that establish the width and depth of the leg notch—repeat the procedure for the back-wing slot.

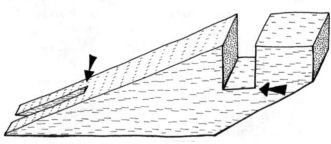

7-8 Arrows show the direction of the fretsaw cuts that link up the slots.

paring cuts, and whittle away the waste on the side quarter nearest your right hand (FIG. 7-10). If you turn the wood from end-to-end and side-to-side, always working the right-hand quarter nearest you, the propeller will gradually take on the characteristic shape. When you are happy with the propeller, use the graded sandpaper to rub the whole thing down to a round edged smooth-to-the-touch finish.

13. When you have achieved a smooth and easy whizz-around fit of the wheels and the propeller with washers on each side of the wood, take them off again, wipe away all the dust and debris, and remove the whole workpiece to the area that you have set aside for painting. Arrange the wheels and the prop on sticks supported in blobs of modeling clay, and pin supports on the underside of the plane so that the paint/varnish is clear of the worksurface.

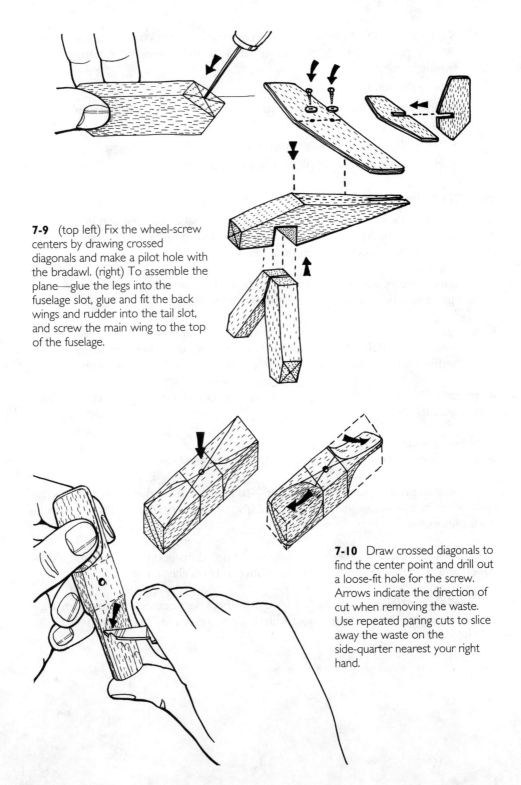

7-9 (top left) Fix the wheel-screw centers by drawing crossed diagonals and make a pilot hole with the bradawl. (right) To assemble the plane—glue the legs into the fuselage slot, glue and fit the back wings and rudder into the tail slot, and screw the main wing to the top of the fuselage.

7-10 Draw crossed diagonals to find the center point and drill out a loose-fit hole for the screw. Arrows indicate the direction of cut when removing the waste. Use repeated paring cuts to slice away the waste on the side-quarter nearest your right hand.

14. Not forgetting to let the paint/varnish dry out between coats, and also to give the dry paint/varnish a swift rubdown with the fine-grade sandpaper, the working order is:

- Give the fuselage, wings, and tail a couple of coats of red acrylic.
- Give the unpainted wheels and the propeller a coat of grain-enhancing varnish.
- Screw the wheels and the propeller back in place.
- Finally, give the whole plane a last coat of varnish.

WATCHPOINTS

When you are choosing your ⅛-inch-thick plywood, make sure that you go for best-quality birch faced multicore. *Note:* A ⅛-inch thickness should contain three/four veneer layers and be perfect faced on both sides.

If, by chance, the edges of the ply are gappy, fill the cavities with a two-tube resin wood filler and sand to a smooth finish before painting.

If you want to cut costs and use up scraps, you could make the wheels and the wings from slightly different thicknesses. For example, the wheels could be ½ inch thick, the front wings ¼ inch thick, the back wings ⅛ inch thick, and so on.

If you can't visualize how the propeller looks, you could use modeling clay to make a prototype to copy.

If you want wing markings, you could stick on letters or numbers cut from a magazine, or you could buy press-on insignia from a model shop.

If you want to make a plane twice the size—10 inches long and 10 inches across the span of the wings—read the scale off as 2 grid squares to 1 inch, and use ¼-inch-thick plywood.

If you decide to make a larger plane, you could use shop-bought wheels and a propeller, and perhaps power the propeller with a rubber/elastic band.

You could hang the plane by a cord from your bedroom ceiling—by an open window—and watch the propeller zoom round. *Be warned:* Don't hammer nails in the ceiling!

8

Sitting ducks

Making a sitting ducks target:

A row of knock-down duck profiles mounted and hinged on a frame.

Primary techniques:

Drawing, compass work, using a fretsaw and tenon saw, drilling holes, cutting notched/lap joints, painting, and fixing hinges.

Age level: 12–13

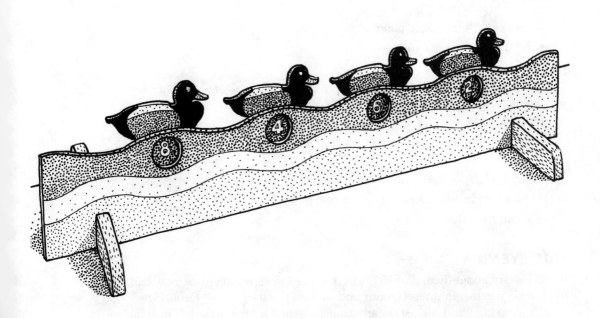

WOODS

- A sheet of best-quality birch-faced ¼-inch-thick multicore plywood at 12 × 36 inches for the wavy facade and the ducks. This allows for cutting waste and for spare.

- A 36-inch length of prepared pine at ½ inch thick and 3 inches wide for the main backing board. This, too, allows for cutting waste.

- A 24-inch length of prepared ½-inch-thick pine at 1½ inches wide, for the two feet.

TOOLS AND MATERIALS

- Crosscut saw
- Small flat-bladed saw, like a tenon or gents
- Coping saw and pack of spare blades
- Workbench with a vice
- Workout paper and a 36-x-6-inch sheet of tracing paper
- Pencil, ruler, and tape measure.
- Compass
- Try square
- Brace drill with a 1½-inch-diameter machine tooth bit to fit
- Bench hook
- Graded sandpaper
- A pack of ⅜-inch-long panel pins
- Small pin/peen hammer
- White PVA glue
- Acrylic paints in *red, black, medium blue, light blue, light green-blue, orange-brown,* and *yellow*
- A sheet of white, rub-on, ¾" numbers (the type used by graphic designers)
- Four brass 1-inch back flap hinges with brass countersunk ⅜-inch-long screws to fit
- Bradawl
- Two paintbrushes: a broad- and a fine-point
- Clear, high-shine varnish

KIDS'-EYE VIEW

Parents worry about them and kids love them: sling-shots, air rifles, bows and arrows, and guns that fire pellets, darts and suckers . . . they are all terrific!

Okay, so guns and sling-shots are dangerous, and it's not good to fire at birds—not good for the birds anyway—so what are you going to fire at? Well, the answer is beautifully simple: What you need is a skill-testing target.

Our Sitting Ducks Target is a great idea. The four ducks are hinged at the back in such a way that when they are hit, they fall down, the numbers flip out of view, and you have scored. This target is good fun to make, even more fun to fire at, and it will put your parents' minds at rest—all in all, a brilliant project!

CAREGIVERS' GUIDE

Making Time and Skill Level—This project focuses in on three woodworking techniques—using a coping saw, cutting a notched lap joint, and fixing hinges with screws. And, of course, once the various forms have been cut and worked, then the imagery needs to be carefully drawn out and painted.

I think it fair to say that the most difficult part of this project is not so much the woodwork—the cutting and drilling—but rather the initial setting out of the curves and images, and the final painting.

A 12–13-year-old—a kid who enjoys woodwork and painting, a kid who is keen to start popping with his/her gun or sling-shot, should be able to get this project made in a weekend.

Cautions and Adult Help—Bearing in mind that older children generally like to be left alone to get on with it, it's best if you are around to help and advise with setting out the design and to help with the final painting. But in between times, take a backstage position and let the kids work it out for themselves. Certainly there is a chance that the kids will make a mess-up, but then again, I think the average 12–13-year-old will safely be able to handle the challenge.

Be Warned—Having established the fact that older children—children who know how to use the tools—need to be left alone, this is not to say that you shouldn't be on standby and ready to help—to hold the wood, to quietly organize the working stages, to clean the brushes, to sweep up the floor, etc. I'm sure you know what I mean!

GETTING DOWN TO WORK

1. Have a look at the project picture (page 83), working drawings (FIGS. 8-1 and 8-2) and the design template (FIG. 8-3) to see how the project is made up from twelve wooden components—the wavy-edged facade board, the 3-inch-wide backing board, the two feet, the four ducks, and the four small pieces of plywood that are pinned on the back of the ducks. Study the layout of the facade board, and note how the position of the dips, curves, and holes has been achieved by dividing the total 30-inch length of the board up into 10 3-inch-wide step-offs (FIG. 8-1, top).

2. When you have a clear understanding of how the target needs to be cut, made, and put together, take your pencil, ruler, try square, and the tracing paper, and draw the facade board and the duck profiles out to full size. Mark in the position of all the details that make up the design.

3. Take the large sheet of ¼-inch plywood and use the crosscut saw to swiftly

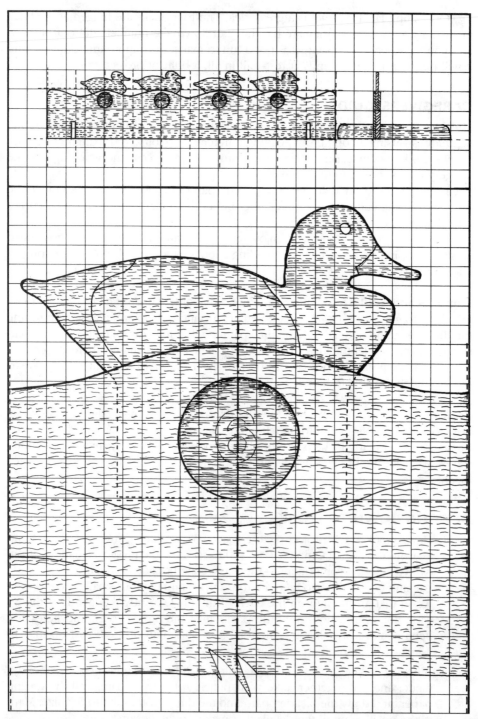

8-1 Working Drawing #1. (top) The scale is approximately 1 grid square to 2 inches. (bottom) The scale is 4 grid squares to 1 inch.

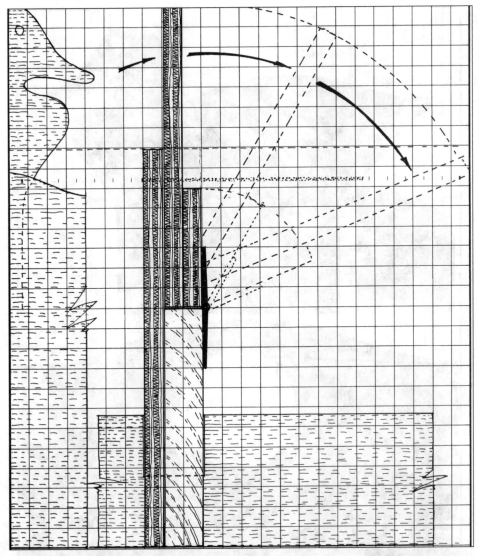

8-2 Working Drawing #2. The scale is 4 grid squares to 1 inch. Note how the duck swings back when it is struck.

cut it down into two 6-inch-wide, 36-inch-long strips. Make sure that the line of cut is clean and straight.

4. Take one of the two plywood strips and the tracing of the facade board, and use the pencil, ruler, square, and the design tracing to carefully pencil-press transfer all the details through to the wood. Remove the tracing paper, and spend time making sure that all the details are correct and clearly marked.

5. Repeat the procedure with the other 6-inch-wide strip of plywood, only this time, of course, transfer the four duck profiles and the four little 3-x-1½-inch

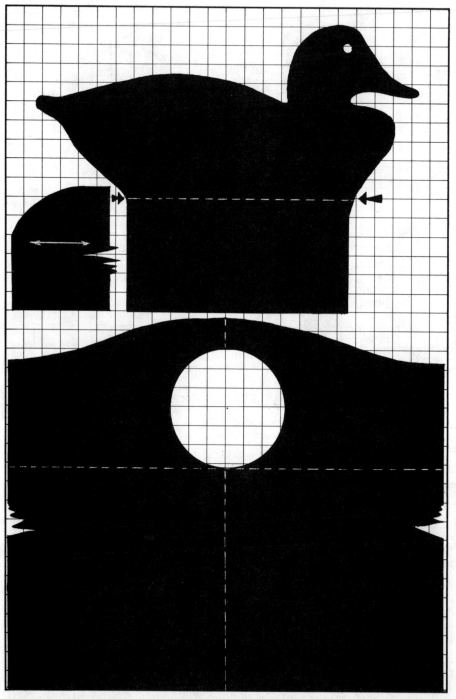

8-3 Design Template. The scale is 4 grid squares to 1 inch. (top left) Detail of foot-end profile. (top right) Duck with the top-of-backplate line arrowed. (bottom) Detail of trough-and-crest facade, with centerline and top-of-backboard line.

backing plates that go behind the ducks (FIG. 8-4). Note, that as there is a generous amount of wood, you could, if you so wish, make another set of ducks for spares.

6. Establish the position of the ducks eyes, and run them through with a small-size drill bit.

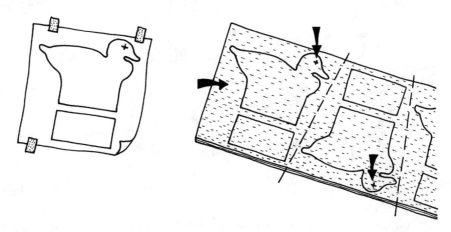

8-4 Trace off the two profiles, mark and drill the ducks eyes, and cut the plywood down into manageable pieces.

7. When you are happy with the transferred shapes—the facade board and the ducks—use the crosscut saw to swiftly cut the wood down into manageable pieces. Then, a piece at a time, set the wood in the vice and use the coping saw to cut out the curves and profiles (FIG. 8-5). When you are using the coping saw, the order of work is:

- Having checked that teeth are pointing away from the handle, adjust the screw-handle so that the blade is well-tensioned.
- Set the workpiece in the vice so that the saw is presented with the line of cut.
- Run the saw at an easy pace, all the while making sure that the cut edge is at right angles to the working face.
- Keep adjusting and moving both the wood and the saw so that the blade is always timely presented with the line of next cut.
- Being careful not to twist and break the blade, work at a steady pace so as not to tear the wood.

Note: A good tip is to cut from the side that's to be painted. Then if the blade does tear the wood, the damage is more likely to be at the back.

8. When you have cut out the wavy-edge facade board, set it best-face-up on the workbench and use the pencil, ruler, and square to re-establish and check the position of the four number holes. If all is correct, the hole centers

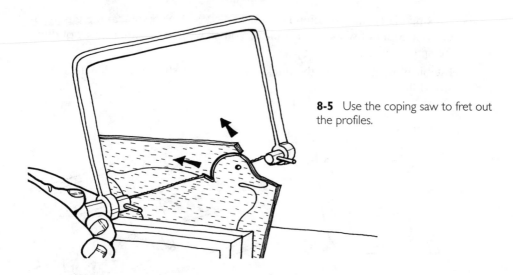

8-5 Use the coping saw to fret out the profiles.

should be set on the 3-inch grid lines, and 1¼ inches down from the top of the peaks (FIG. 8-3).

9. Having fixed the position of the four holes, clamp the facade board firm-down on the bench over some scrap wood, and use the brace drill and the 1½-inch-diameter machine tooth bit to bore the holes through (FIG. 8-6).

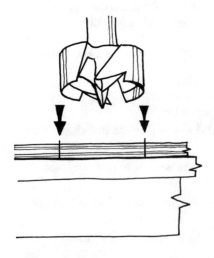

8-6 Use the brace and the 1½-inch-diameter machine tooth bit to bore out the score-number holes.

10. While you are working on the facade board, take the pencil, ruler, and square, and draw out the two ½-inch-wide, ¾-inch-deep foot notches. If all is correct, the notches should be set 3 inches in from each end of the board.

11. Take the 24-inch length of prepared ½-inch-thick 1½-inch-wide wood (the bit for the feet), cut it down into two 12-inch lengths, and then use the pencil,

ruler, compass, and square to draw out the end curves and to fix the position of the facade board location notches (FIG. 8-7).

12. When you are happy with the shape of the curves and the position of the notches, set the wood in the vice and use the tenon saw and the coping saw to cut the joints and curves. The curves are easy enough: You just run the coping saw blade around a little to the waste side of the drawn line so that the cut edge is at right angles to the working face. The notches are a little more tricky, in that you first have to establish the depth and width of the notch with the tenon saw (FIG. 8-8, top), and then clear the waste with the coping saw (FIG. 8-8, bottom).

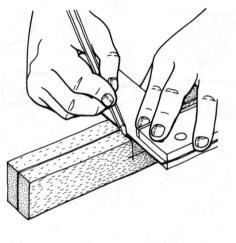

8-7 (top) Use the pencil and square to fix the position of the facade board location notches. (bottom) Use the pencil and compass to draw out the 1-inch radius end curves. The arrows show the position of the compass point.

13. Take the 36-inch length of 3-inch-wide wood (the piece for the backing board), and cut it down in length so that it checks out with the facade board. Support the workpiece hard up against the bench hook (FIG. 8-9). Having checked for fit, smear a small amount of glue on mating faces, clamp together and pin-fix the two boards together by nailing through from the best face of the facade board. A good tip is to disguise the pins by placing them so that they occur along one of the wavy paint lines. Remove the clamps, and cut the two notch joints as already described, so that the feet are a nice tight-push notch-to-notch fit.

14. Take the duck profiles one at a time, pair them up with the little 3-x-1½-inch backing plates, and glue and pin-fix. Make sure that the plates are fixed to the back of the ducks so that when all four ducks are in place, they look to be swimming from left-to-right. Have the fixing pins placed at the corners so that they are well away from the hinge area (FIG. 8-10).

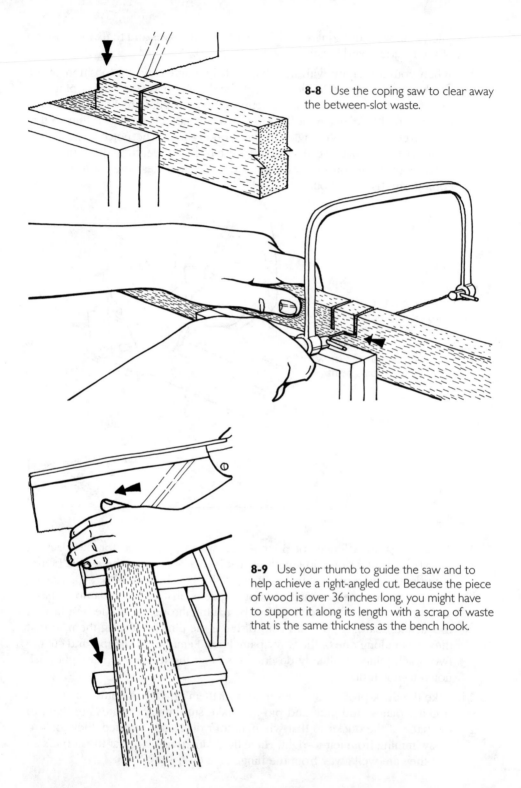

8-8 Use the coping saw to clear away the between-slot waste.

8-9 Use your thumb to guide the saw and to help achieve a right-angled cut. Because the piece of wood is over 36 inches long, you might have to support it along its length with a scrap of waste that is the same thickness as the bench hook.

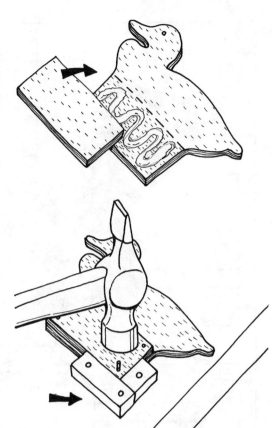

8-10 Glue the backing plate to the back of the duck, then brace them against the bench stop and carefully pin them at the four corners.

15. When the glue is dry, rub all the components down to a smooth slightly round-edged finish, wipe away the dust, and move them to the area set aside for painting.

16. Having drawn and traced all the design details up to full size, pencil-press transfer all the imagery through to the wood. Then take your brushes and paints, and set to work blocking in all the areas of color (FIG. 8-11). Don't try for fussy realistic imagery; it's much better to stay with the stylized blocks of color—that is, with each area of color being clean-edged, sharply defined, and flat. (*Note:* Follow the photograph in the color insert as a guide.) The color guide is as follows:

    • Black for the duck's head and tail

    • Brown and blue for the wings

    • Yellow for the bill

    • Red for the behind-circle number area

    First paint the outline with the fine-point brush, then fill in with the larger brush. Don't forget to paint the ply edges.

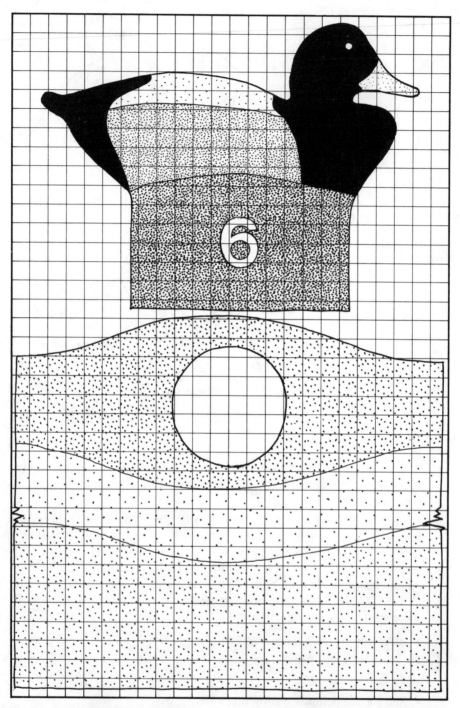

8-11 Painting grid. The scale is 4 grid squares to 1 inch. The bill is yellow, the number area red, the head and tail black, the top-of-back gray-blue, the wings brown, the top of the wave a medium dark blue, the middle wave pale blue, and the bottom of the facade another shade of blue.

Children ages 7 to 8 will not only enjoy making these matchbox-sized boats, they also will find them perfect for bathtime fun.

The monkey imagery used in this memo holder makes it a delightful addition to a child's desk. With supervision, a 10- or 11-year-old can easily finish this project in a weekend.

This castle, a great project for 8- and 9-year olds, can pack flat for easy carrying.

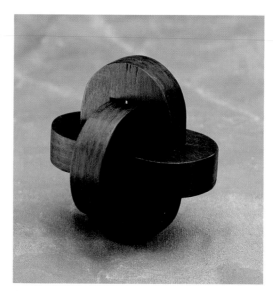

Fourteen- to fifteen-year-olds will find a challenge in this Japanese wooden puzzle. (Don't worry—directions for solving the puzzle are included!)

This wooden airplane has wheels and a propeller. It's both a fun toy and a good woodworking project for children aged 11 to 12.

Children ages 10 to 11 will enjoy making and using this witty door knocker. Creating this project will increase their woodworking skills and putting it on their bedroom door will help them feel they have a "private" place.

What child wouldn't have fun with this whizz-around propeller toy? It's a fun project for 10- to 11-year-olds.

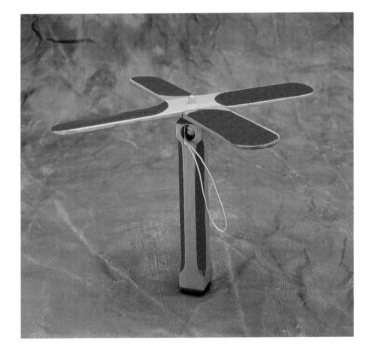

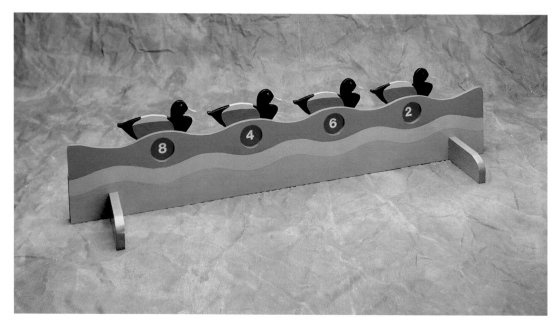

Kids will love using these "sitting ducks" for target practice! A good project for 12-year-olds.

Let kids show their patriotic spirit with this American eagle letter holder. For older kids (ages 14 to 15), this project will show off their more-advanced woodworking skills.

17. When the acrylic paints are dry, take the sheet of rub-on numbers and set each duck out with a suitable score number. The easiest way is to establish the number area by setting the duck in place and then to pencil in the circle by using the cutout circle as a stencil template. *Note:* We have gone for large-size single-digit numbers because they are easier to place and clearer to see.

18. One duck at a time, mark in the center-of-duck line, set the duck in position on the top edge of the backing board, and align the backflap hinge with the centerline. Make screw-starter holes with the bradawl (FIG. 8-12), and then screw-fix the hinges in place. Drive the top and bottom screws in first, and then follow through with the others. *Note:* The screws need to be no longer than ⅜ inch in length.

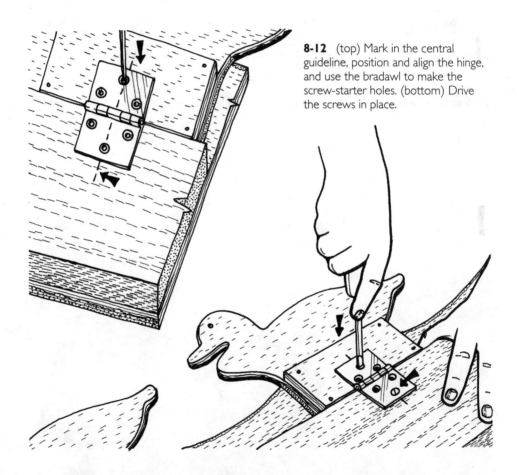

8-12 (top) Mark in the central guideline, position and align the hinge, and use the bradawl to make the screw-starter holes. (bottom) Drive the screws in place.

19. Finally, noting that the longest part of the feet is to the back, set the target on its two notched, round-ended feet and give it a couple of all-over coats of clear, high-shine varnish. A good tip when varnishing is to view the workpiece with a strong side light so that you can easily spot missed areas and dribbles. Now the ducks are ready for popping!

WATCHPOINTS

If you like the idea of the target, but want to make it larger in size or longer, then all you need to do is to scale up the size accordingly. If you do decide to make the ducks, say, twice the size, then you might need to use thicker plywood and larger hinges.

Bearing in mind that in time air rifle shot/pellets will damage the ducks, you could make a spare replacement set, or you could face the ducks with tinplate.

If you can get to use a scroll saw, you could speed up the project by cutting the ducks out in multiples of six or more at a time.

If you haven't got a large-size bit for the large circles, cut them out with a fretsaw.

If you like the idea of the target, but are not so keen on having animal imagery, you could go for a simple geometrical shape.

Be Warned: When you are using the target, make sure that it is set up against a large windowless, doorless wall or fence.

9
Showplace

Making a console shelf:

A half-circle shelf with an ornamental bracket.

Primary techniques:

Fretting, drilling, screw-jointing, painting, and distressing.

Age level: 13–14

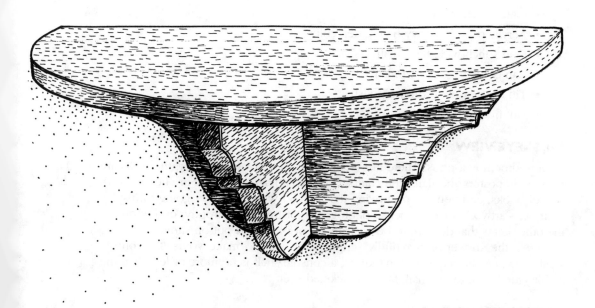

WOODS

- A plank of prepared ¾-inch-thick wood at 48 inches long and 9½ inches wide—best to use an easy-to-work wood like white pine or parana pine.

Note: If you want to cut costs, you could make the shelf up from off-cuts of different thicknesses. For example, it wouldn't matter too much if the shelf were ¾ inch thick and the bracket ½ inch thick. However, it is important to choose a straight-grained length of wood. If it's full of knots or splits, then it's going to be a problem.

TOOL AND MATERIALS

- Electric scroll saw
- Workbench with vice
- Workout and tracing paper
- Pencil and ruler
- Try square
- Small straight saw
- A pair of compasses or dividers (with a leg stretch of at least 9 inches)
- Hand drill with a selection of bits to fit
- Six 1¾-inch-long countersunk screws
- Screwdriver to fit screws
- Graded sandpaper
- Acrylic paint in an ivy blue-green color
- One 1-inch-wide flat brush
- Can of matte sheen varnish
- Tin of beeswax furniture polish
- Lint-free polishing cloth

KIDS'-EYE VIEW

Your bedroom is a mess! There are clothes spread all over the floor, the walls are covered in posters and flags, the chairs, bedside cabinet, and chest are heaped with school books, and you are occupying the bed. So where are you going to display your class artwork, or that special photograph, or the sports trophy, or any one of the other items that deserve to be given pride of place and put on show?

Well, the answer is beautifully simple. You need to make yourself a console shelf. Now, just in case you don't know, a console shelf is no more or less than the architectural term for a small, fancy, bracketed shelf.

CAREGIVERS' GUIDE

Making Time and Skill Level—Although the end result is quite a fancy piece of woodwork, I would say that the making stages are relatively easy and manageable. An average 14- to 15-year-old will have this project made, put together, and decorated in about 8–10 hours.

Cautions and Adult Help—The putting together is a bit tricky, but only because the shapes need to be held secure while the screws are being driven home. Best to offer help and be around when it comes to putting various components together.

If the child is going to use an electric scroll saw, then you need to have your wits about you and be ready for the unexpected. Be careful not to over-tension the blade, make sure the ON/OFF switch is working and within reach, and generally make sure that the working area is safe. Keep an eye open, and watch over the child.

Be Warned—When a scroll saw blade breaks, it's a noisy but harmless business. Be ready with a pack of spare blades.

GETTING DOWN TO WORK

1. Have a look at the project picture (page 97), the working drawing (FIG. 9-1) and the design template (FIG. 9-2), and see how the console shelf is made up from three components—a backboard, a bracket board, and a half-circle shelf. See how, at a grid scale of 4 grid squares to 3 inches, the shelf is 18 inches long, 9 inches deep, and 7¾ inches high. Note the direction of the grain, the position of the various drilled holes, and the way the bracket board is the same size and shape as half of the backboard.

2. Have a look at the wood and make sure that it is free from stains, loose knots, and splits. If there are any problems, then now is the time to consider choosing another piece.

3. Draw the design up to full size. Make a careful tracing of the back and bracket boards, and pencil-press transfer the traced lines through to the wood. Use the try square to make sure that the straight sides of the two boards are aligned with the straight sides of the plank (FIG. 9-3).

4. Set the dividers/compass to a radius of 9 inches, spike the point on the centerline on one edge of the plank, and scribe out the 18-inch-diameter half-circle that makes up the shelf (FIG. 9-4).

5. When you are happy with the shape of the transferred images, take the straight saw and swiftly cut the wood down into three easy-to-handle pieces. Now switch on the scroll saw and start fretting out the profiles. Using the scroll saw is easy and safe, as long as you work at a steady even pace, hold the wood firm-down on the cutting table, and run the wood into the moving blade so that the line of cut is slightly to the waste side of the drawn line (FIG. 9-5).

6. When you have achieved the three boards, take the graded sandpaper and rub all the shaped sawn edges down to a slightly rounded smooth-to-the-touch finish. Leave the straight edges clean-cut and sharp-cornered.

7. Use a pencil and ruler to check and perhaps re-establish the various fitting lines on the three boards—the centerlines on the half-circle shelf and the backboard, and the thickness of the backboard on the straight edge of the shelf.

8. Having seen how the three boards fit together in relationship to each other, mark in the position of the eight screw holes. There should be two holes

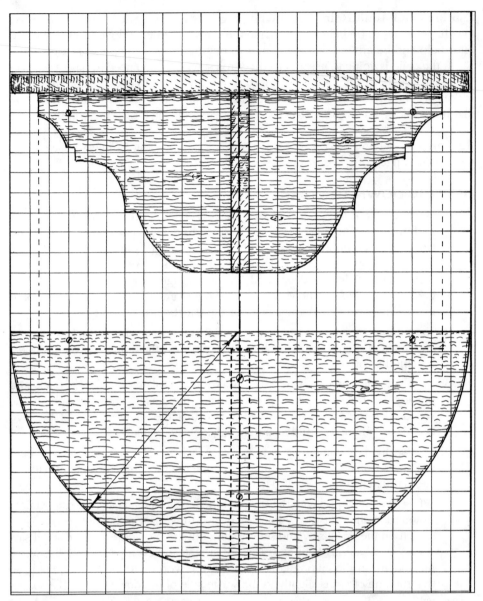

9-1 Working Drawing. At a scale of about 4 grid squares to 3 inches, the shelf is 18 inches long, 9 inches deep, and 7¾ inches high. (top) Front view. (bottom) Plan view.

through the backboard centerline, two holes through the half-circle shelf centerline, two holes set about ⅜ inch in from the straight edge of the shelf, and two hanging holes through the backboard.

9. When you have checked and double-checked the position of the holes, choose a bit diameter to suit the size of your screws—meaning the diameter of the shanks—and then, with the hand drill, carefully run all the holes

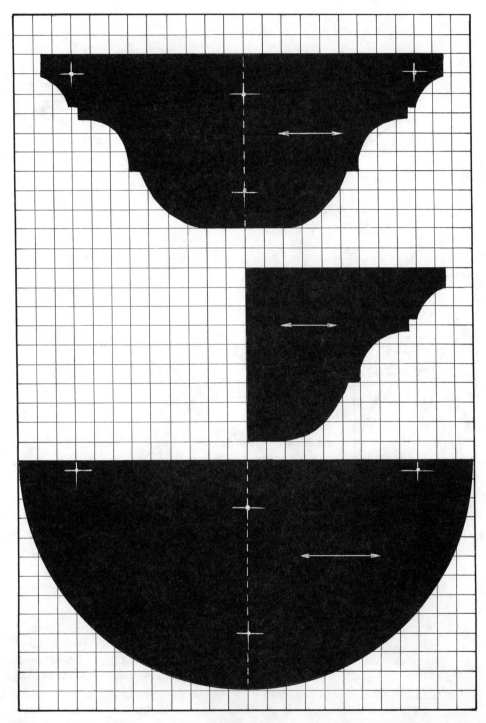

9-2 Design Template. The scale is 4 grid squares to 3 inches. Note the position of the screw holes and the direction of the grain.

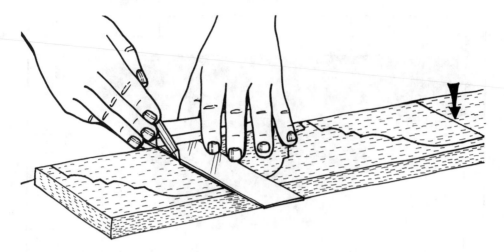

9-3 Use the try square to make sure that the straight sides of the boards are at right angles to the sides of the prepared plank.

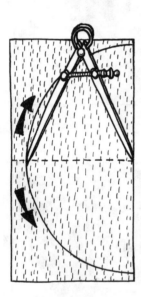

9-4 Follow the direction of the arrows to scribe out the 18-inch-diameter half-circle.

through. Follow up with the countersink bit, and countersink drill all surface holes so as to allow for the head of the screws (FIG. 9-6). *Note:* Bear in mind when you are screw-fixing two bits of wood together that the top hole needs to be a loose fit clearance for the shank (See *screws* in Beginner's Guide).

10. With the bracket board secured back-edge-uppermost in the vice, dribble a small amount of glue on mating surfaces of the backboard, and set it down in position so that the centerline is aligned and square. Run two screws through the backboard and into the bracket (FIG. 9-7).

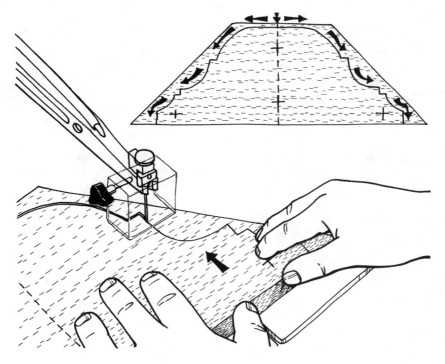

9-5 Start at the centerline and follow the arrows to cut one side of the board at a time.

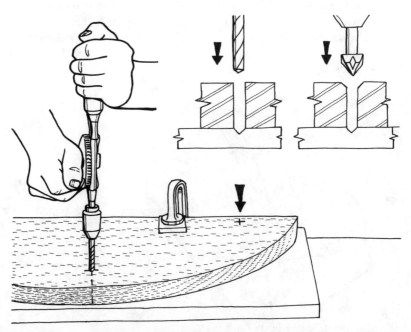

9-6 Secure the half-circle shelf on scrap wood to the bench, and drill out the initial screw-clearance holes.

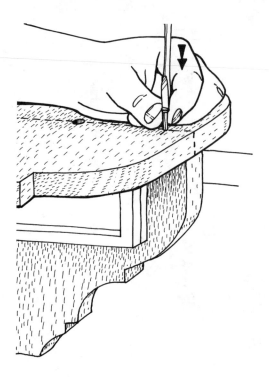

9-7 With the bracket board secured in the vice and the backboard carefully aligned, dribble a small amount of glue on mating surfaces, and run screws through the backboard clearance holes and on into the bracket.

11. Set the backboard flat-down on the bench and against a bench stop so that the bracket board is standing at right angles to the worksurface, and position the half-circle shelf. When you are happy with the arrangement, clamp the wood securely or get a friend/adult to hold the wood, and run four screws through the shelf—two into the top edge of the backboard and two into the back edge of the bracket (FIG. 9-8).

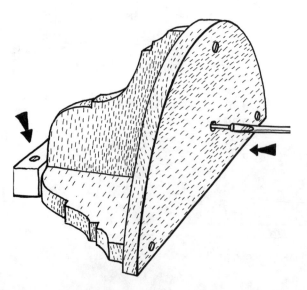

9-8 Set the backboard flat-down on the bench and against the bench stop, dribble a small amount of glue on mating surfaces, position and align the half-circle shelf, and run screws into the backboard and the bracket.

12. Wipe away all the dust and debris, stir the green paint, and give the whole workpiece—back, front, and sides—a couple of thin, well-brushed coats (FIG. 9-9, top).

13. When the paint is completely dry, take a piece of fine-grade sandpaper and rub the workpiece down to a smooth finish. Cut through the paint on the edges and corners so that the shelf takes on an old, much-handled folk-art look (FIG. 9-9, bottom).

14. Brush away the dust and give the workpiece a thin coat of matte sheen varnish.

15. When the varnish is dry, wipe the whole thing over with a generous amount of beeswax polish and burnish the wood to a deep, dull-sheen finish.

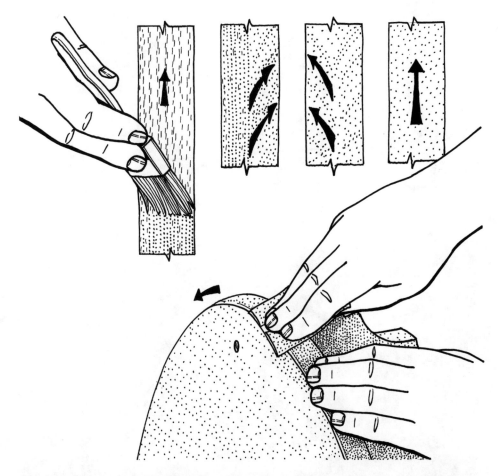

9-9 Always try to work with the grain of the wood when painting. To prevent runs at the edges, first use a single-stroke action to cover the edge, then stroke from center to sides, and finally wipe away the runs with a single through stroke.

WATCHPOINTS

If you are a beginner, it might be a good idea to have a couple of practice runs on the scroll saw before you start cutting out the special wood. Draw out a couple of circles on some scrap wood and see if you can run the line of cut a little to waste side of the drawn line.

You could go for a more complex design and use a housing joint to join the bracket to the backboard.

If you don't want the screw heads to show, you could bore out the countersink holes and cover the screw heads with dowels/plugs. (See Beginner's Guide.)

Making a steerable two-seater sled:

A sledge or sled with a bolt-pivoted steerable front section.

Primary techniques:

Sawing, planing, drilling, dovetail jointing, half-lap jointing, shaping, finishing, and painting.

Age level: 13–14

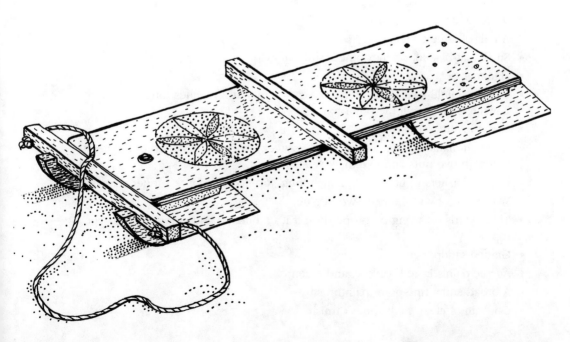

WOODS

- A 40-inch length of prepared wood at 9 inches wide and 1 inch thick to be cut in half for the two cross-runner boards. Best to use a nice bit of straight-grained pine.
- An 80-inch length of wood for the four runners. Bear in mind when you are choosing your wood that the runners need to be strong. Avoid wood that looks to be split, knotty, or warped.
- A 60-inch length of 2-x-2-inch-square section wood to be cut in half for the two cross-bar foot bracers.
- A sheet of best-quality exterior-grade 1-inch-thick plywood at 60 inches long and 18 inches wide for the top board.

TOOLS AND MATERIALS

- General-purpose crosscut or panel-type saw
- Tenon saw
- Coping saw
- One medium-size clamp
- Eight large clamps
- Workbench with vice
- A 1-inch-wide beveled chisel
- Brace/hand drill with countersink
- A selection of bits to fit drill
- Pencil, ruler, and try square
- Marking knife and marking gauge
- Workout and tracing paper
- A pair of large dividers
- Small, flat-bladed, open-toothed, surform rasp.
- Hammer
- Twelve stainless-steel countersunk screws: two at 2½ inches long and ten at 2 inches long for all the other fixings.
- Screwdrivers to fit screws
- A ½-inch-diameter 3-inch-long stainless-steel hex-head or slotted dome-head bolt with two nuts and five thick washers to fit.
- Fifteen washers to fit the five 2-inch-long, top-board-to-back runner screws.
- Waterproof, two-tube resin wood glue.
- Three yards of strong pull-rope (best if it's a braided and colored yacht-type rope)
- Graded sandpaper
- Acrylic paints in red, yellow, and green
- A broad and a fine-point paintbrush
- One can of clear, high-shine varnish

KIDS'-EYE VIEW

Just imagine: The long-range weather forecast predicts lots and lots of snow. You are going to wake up in a day or so and the whole world will be blanketed in white. The roads will be blocked, the school will be closed down, and just about everything will come to a halt. It's going to be real cool and white out—what fun! So don't be left out; now is the time to get busy with the woodwork and build yourself a two-seater steerable sled.

Just think, when all your friends are stuck indoors, you will be able to go out into the white world and have a rare old time. You will be able to zoom down hills, run into snow drifts, take groceries to stranded old folks, sell rides to the kids next door, and generally have a ball.

CAREGIVER'S GUIDE

Making Time and Skill Level—This project is not so much difficult as it is lengthy. There are four runners, four edge-lap dovetail joints, lots of curves to be cut, two half-laps, and so on. You will need to be organized, and the kids will need to be well motivated.

This is a really good group project for a family or a club. I would say that a 13- to 14-year-old working alongside an adult could have this sled made and ready to zoom in a week of evenings or a long weekend.

Cautions and Adult Help—The success of this project hinges on the four dovetail joints being cut and worked so that they are a good, tight fit. This being so, you will have to be around to guide the kids in the right direction. If they are experienced woodworkers, you shouldn't have any problems.

If, on the other hand, the kids are raw beginners, then it might be a good idea to have a try-out with some scrap wood. This is one of those projects where you will have to weigh up the situation—the ability, the tools, the materials, and the motivation—and use your judgment.

Be Warned—As the children might well be working in a group, and taking into account that they are perhaps overexcited at the prospect of using the sled, you will have to keep a tight rein on proceedings and see to it that tasks are carefully and safely allotted. A younger child could watch an older brother or sister, another child could be given the easier sawing tasks, an older child could cut the joints, and so on. Consider the space and the tools, and then think the problems through accordingly.

GETTING DOWN TO WORK

1. Have a look at the project picture (page 107), working drawings (FIG. 10-1) and the design template (FIG. 10-2), and see how the sled is made up from nine primary component parts—the four runner boards, the two cross-runner boards, the large plywood top board, and the two cross-bar foot-bracers. Because the pivot bolt that runs through the top board and the cross-runner board has a washer at top and bottom and three large washers between the

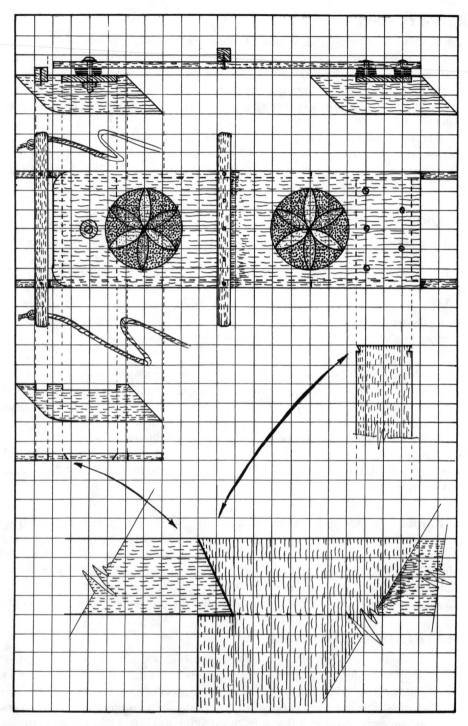

10-1 Working Drawing and Painting grid. (top) The scale is 1 grid square to 3 inches. (bottom) The scale of the dovetail detail is 4 grid squares to 1 inch.

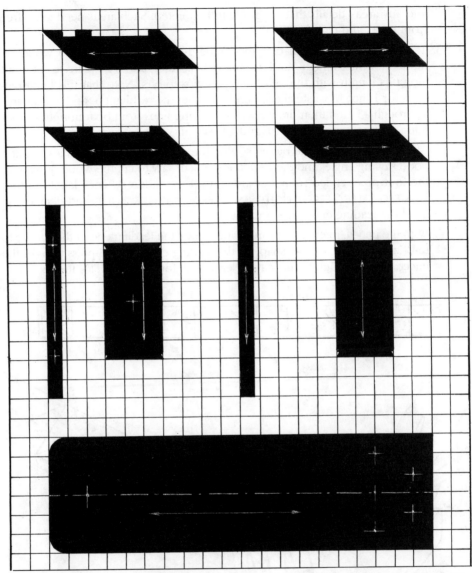

10-2 Design Template. The scale is 1 grid square to 3 inches. Note the run of the grain and the position of the various screw and bolt holes.

two boards to act as a bearing, it is necessary to pack washers between the top board and the back runners.

Note also how the top board has been decorated with a couple of easy-to-do, compass-worked, decorative hex motifs. Draw the design up to full size.

2. When you have a clear understanding of how the parts need to be made and put together, set the wood out on the workbench and check it over to make sure that it is in good condition. Pay particular attention to the runner wood,

and any areas/details that are going to be jointed. Such areas need to be free from knots and damage.

3. Take the 80-inch length of 6-inch-wide 1-inch-thick wood—the wood intended for the runners—and use the pencil, ruler, and try square to set it out along its length with thirteen 6-inch-wide step-offs. Note that this length allows for 1 inch of waste at each end. Number the resultant 6-x-6-inch squares 1 through 13, and then draw diagonal cutting lines from bottom-right to top-left across squares 1, 4, 7, 10, and 13 (FIG. 10-3, top).

4. Clamp the wood on the bench so that the diagonal cutting lines are set at a good sawing angle, and then use the crosscut saw to cut the wood down into the four point-ended runner boards (FIG. 10-3, middle). Pencil label the runners FRONT LEFT, FRONT RIGHT, BACK LEFT, and BACK RIGHT, and decide and label the leading end of each runner.

5. With the pencil, ruler, and tracing paper, draw the leading end of the runner to full size, and establish the shape of the leading curve. Pencil-press transfer the traced curve through to the leading end of all four runners (FIG. 10-3, bottom).

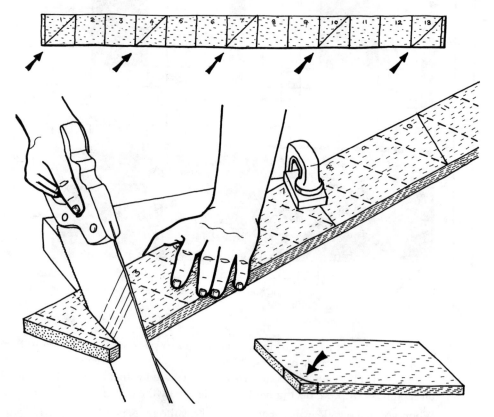

10-3 Draw diagonal cutting lines from bottom-right to top-left across squares (1, 4, 7, 10, and 13). Clamp the wood down on the bench and use the crosscut saw to cut the four point-ended runner boards, then draw the shape of the leading curve on each runner.

6. When you have drawn the curve out on all four runners, secure one runner ground-edge-uppermost in the vice, and use the rasp to cut away the waste and to take the curve to a good finish. Make sure that you work in the direction of the grain—that is, from the ground edge of the runner, and over and around the curve and on towards the leading point (FIG. 10-4).

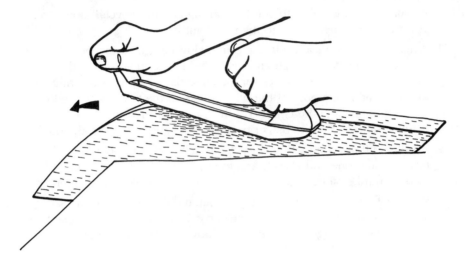

10-4 Use the rasp to remove the waste.

7. Take the 40-inch length of 9-inch-wide, 1-inch-thick wood—the piece for the two cross-runner boards—and allowing for end waste, use the pencil, ruler, marking knife, and try square to set out the two 18-inch-long boards. Cut the wood to size and trim off the end waste.

8. Measure 1 inch in from the end of the board, ½ inch in from the end-edge, and run a diagonal across the resultant 1-x-½-inch rectangle, so as to set out the flare of the first dovetail. Repeat this procedure on all corners of both boards, and then remove each little triangle of waste with two well placed straight cuts of the tenon saw (FIG. 10-5). Pencil label the boards/ends FRONT LEFT, FRONT RIGHT and so on.

9. Set the FRONT LEFT runner top-edge-uppermost in the jaws of the vice, and use the pencil, ruler, marking knife, marking gauge, and the dovetail shape on the FRONT LEFT cross-runner board dovetail, to mark in the shape of the dovetail housing. Set the marking gauge at 1 inch, strike off the depth of the housing, and use the dovetail ends of the cross-runner board to check the flared shape on the top edge. Shade in the area of waste (FIG. 10-6, left).

Note: From left to right, the joints need to be identical but mirror-imaged.

10. Still with the runner set top-edge-uppermost in the vice, the order of work for cutting the dovetail housing is:
    - Being sure to stay to the waste side of scored lines, fix the shape of the joint and break up the grain along the length of the waste by taking the

tenon saw and running half a dozen cuts down through the edge of the board.

- Use the coping saw to remove the bulk of the waste (FIG. 10-6, bottom).
- Use the bevel-edged chisel to carefully lower the waste at the ends and edges of the housing.
- Finally, use the chisel to cut the housing and the dovetail down to a tight flush-fit, and then go on to the next joint.

11. When you have cut and fitted the four dovetails, take the pencil, ruler, try square, and marking gauge and mark the notched joint in on the two front runners (meaning the notches for the cross-bar foot-bracer steering bar). Set the width and the depth of the notch out with the tenon saw, and then use the coping saw and the chisel (FIG. 10-7) to cut away the joint in the way already described. Cut the bracer bars to length and check for a good fit.

12. Take the 60-inch-long, 18-inch-wide, 1-inch-thick top board, label the best face TOP and one end FRONT, and then use the dividers set to a radius of 3 inches to strike off the two quarter-circle arcs that make the front end profile.

13. With the front curve corners nicely set out, use the saw, rasp, and sandpapers to cut away the waste and shape the curve. Use a block and sandpaper to rub all the faces and edges of the plywood down to a smooth splinter-free finish.

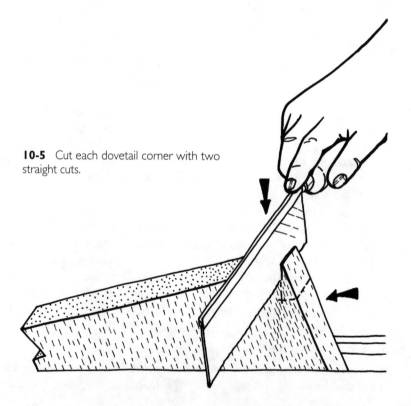

10-5 Cut each dovetail corner with two straight cuts.

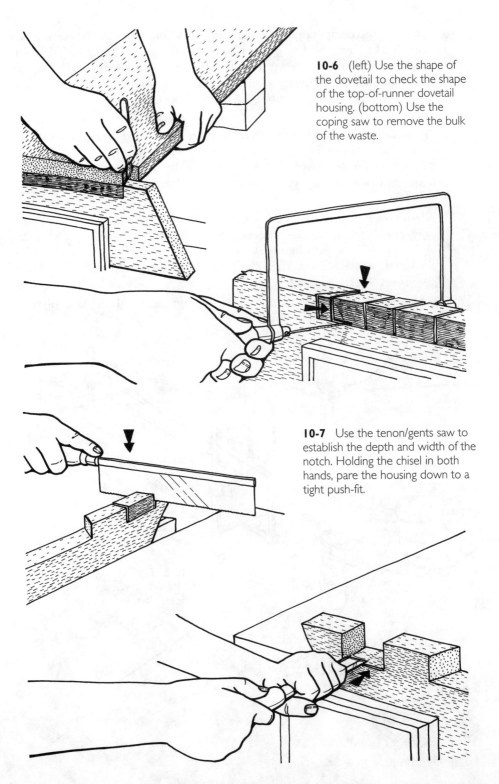

10-6 (left) Use the shape of the dovetail to check the shape of the top-of-runner dovetail housing. (bottom) Use the coping saw to remove the bulk of the waste.

10-7 Use the tenon/gents saw to establish the depth and width of the notch. Holding the chisel in both hands, pare the housing down to a tight push-fit.

14. Collect all the components together and spread them out on the workbench. You should have the four runner boards with all the joints cut, the front cross-bar foot-bracer steering bar, the passenger foot-bracer bar, the two dovetail-ended cross-runner boards, and the plywood top board, all variously jointed, cut to length, and rubbed down to a good finish.

15. Having run your eye over the working drawing (FIG. 10-1), fix the position of the bolt-pivot hole on the front cross-runner board by drawing crossed diagonals, and establish the pivot hole on the centerline of the top board by measuring 6 inches along from the front end. Use the drill and a bit that is slightly larger in diameter than your chosen bolt to bore out the pivot holes (FIG. 10-8, left).

16. When you are ready to put the sled together, start by mixing a small amount of resin glue and fitting the runners to the cross-boards. Be generous with the glue. Tap the dovetails into their housings, and make sure that the runners are square to the boards. Then clamp up and put them to one side until the glue is set (FIG. 10-8, right).

17. Set the runners down on the bench and bridge them with the long plywood

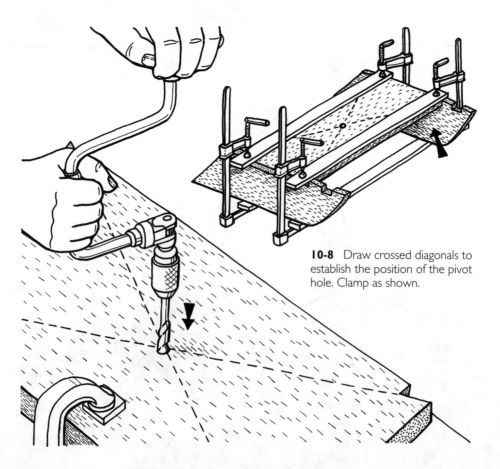

10-8 Draw crossed diagonals to establish the position of the pivot hole. Clamp as shown.

top board. Slide the stainless-steel bolt down through the front board-runner pivot hole and on through the cross-runner hole. With a washer at top and bottom and three washers between mating boards, grease the washers so that the pivot is a smooth and easy fit, and lock the whole works in place with the two nuts (FIG. 10-9, left).

18. Align the back end of the top board with the back runners, and clamp in place. Drill clearance holes through the top board, countersink the holes, and then—with three packing washers per screw between mating boards—screw-fix the top board to the cross-runner board.

19. Take the front foot-bracer steering bar and bore out rope holes that are about 2–3 inches in from each end. Mark the centers where the bar rests in the notches, and drill clearance and countersink holes for the screws (FIG. 10-9, right). Glue and screw the bar in place across the two front runners. Clamp the middle foot bar in place across the width of the top board, turn the sled upside down, and drill and screw through the top board and through to the bar.

20. Finally, use the compass/dividers set to a radius of 6 inches to draw out the two decorative hex circle stars (FIG. 10-1). Block the design in with the acrylic paints, wait awhile for the paint to dry, and then give the sled a couple of generous coats of clear varnish. Tie and knot the cord onto the front foot bar, and the sled is ready for action.

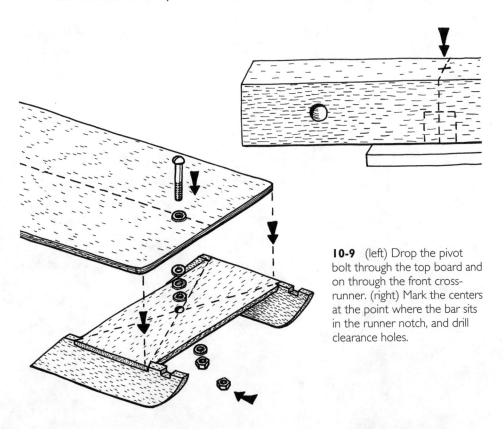

10-9 (left) Drop the pivot bolt through the top board and on through the front cross-runner. (right) Mark the centers at the point where the bar sits in the runner notch, and drill clearance holes.

WATCHPOINTS

If you want stronger joints on the runners, you could use thicker wood for the cross-runner boards and cut shoulder on the dovetails.

If you don't much like the idea of using plywood for the top board, you could use three 6-inch-wide boards set and glued side by side.

If you would like to simplify the design and use only one wood size, you could build the whole sled from 6-x-1-inch cross-section wood.

If your workshop doesn't run to eight large clamps, you could do one dovetail joint at a time and settle for two clamps.

You could strengthen the runners by screw-fixing metal strip—brass, stainless steel or aluminum—along the ground-edge of the runners.

If you think you might want to lie flat-out on the sled, then you could have the passenger's foot bracer bar set on the underside of the top board.

A clever angle

Making a portable drafting unit:

An angled drawing board that incorporates a carry handle.

Primary techniques:

Drawing, compass work, using a crosscut saw and a coping saw, paring with a chisel, drilling holes, fitting hinges, and sanding.

Age level: 14–15

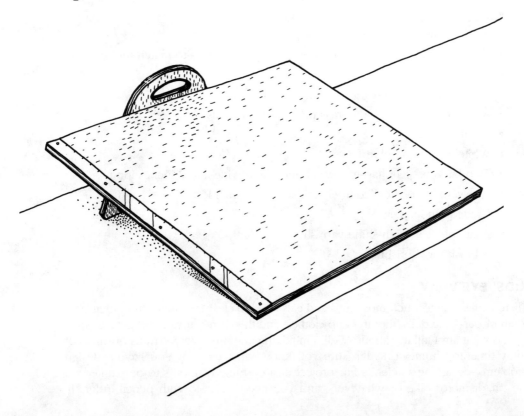

WOODS

- A quarter-sheet of best-quality ½-inch-thick birch-faced multicore plywood at 24 × 48 inches. This allows for a small amount of cutting waste.

TOOLS AND MATERIALS

- Crosscut saw
- Coping saw with spare blades
- Workbench with vice
- Workout and tracing paper
- Pencil and ruler
- Compass and T-square
- Try square
- Small hand drill with small-diameter bits and a set of countersinks
- Craft knife
- A 1-inch-wide bevel-edged chisel
- Clamp
- One brass or steel flat-faced ruler (will be attached to the drafting unit)
- Hacksaw
- Smooth-cut file
- Small, metalworker's center-point punch
- Five ⅜-inch-long countersunk screws—brass or steel—to match the ruler
- Bradawl
- Screwdriver to fit screws
- A handful of ¾-inch-long brass pins, nails, or brads
- Small hammer
- White PVA wood glue
- Two brass or steel flap-hinges, about ¾ inch wide and 2 inches long
- Twelve brass or steel countersunk screws (¾ inch long)
- Graded sandpaper
- A can of clear, high-shine varnish
- A brush for varnishing

KIDS'-EYE VIEW

There comes a time when most guys and gals need to clear the clutter from their bedroom or den—the dolls, the dress-up clothes, and the Disney toys—and get serious.

So what am I talking about? Well, I'm talking about the very serious business of study time and homework. I'm sure you know what I mean! You have a design problem—designing a science fair project or a costume or motifs to be painted on the car or motor bike or whatever—and you need to set-to with pencil, ruler, T-square, and compass, and get it all down on paper. You stare at the large, empty sheet of paper . . . Your brain goes dead, your mind wanders, your eyes mist over, and then—before you can say Frank Lloyd Wright, Andy Whats-his-name, and Richard Buckminster Fuller—the ideas start coming, and the paper is a mass of incredibly exciting sketches, workout designs, and images.

Okay, so this drafting board won't turn you into a designer-artist genius—no sir! But it will ease away all the backaches and headaches. It presents the drawing at a good angle, it has one true runner just in case you need to use a T- square, it is portable, and it looks good. This drafting board will give you the professional edge that will put you one step ahead.

CAREGIVERS' GUIDE

Making Time and Skill Level—Although on the face of it this is one of those projects that requires a minimum of technique know-how—just a bit of careful measuring, a small amount of sawing and paring, and not much else—it is, in fact, a tricky project that needs to be managed with extra care and attention to detail. Because the board has to do with drafting, artwork, and design, all the more reason why the finished board needs to be clean, crisp, and functional. If this project is to be a success, the wood must be kept clean and free from dents, and the curves must be smooth.

That said, a well-motivated 14- to 15-year-old—a teenager who enjoys art and design—should be able to get this project made in a long weekend.

Cautions and Adult Help—This project pivots (both literally and metaphorically) on the two components—the drawing board and the composite handle-stand—being precisely hinged together. If the half-circle hinge-plates are badly placed, or if the hinges are badly fitted, then the project will be a mess-up.

It's not so easy to help the average 14- to 15-year-old. The best that you can do is to talk the project over, provide the materials, make sure that the tools are in good condition, and generally see to it that the working environment is clean and uncluttered.

Be Warned—A warped, dented, and wonky drawing board is worse than useless. This being so, be extra mindful about using smooth pieces of scrap under the clamps, and on keeping the worksurface free from grit and debris.

GETTING DOWN TO WORK

1. Have a good long look at the project picture (page 119), the working drawings (FIGS. 11-1, 11-2, and 11-3) and the design template (FIG. 11-4), and see how the drawing board drafting unit is made up from four plywood components—the drawing surface at 28 × 20 inches, the A-shaped handle-stand, and the two 6-inch-diameter half-circle hinge-plates. See the way the handle-stand can be hinged flat to make an easy-to-hold handle, or opened out at 90° to the drawing surface so as to make a stand. Note also how a 24-inch store-bought metal ruler has been cut to length and inlaid into the edge of the board so that it is flush with the working surface.

2. When you have studied the drawings in all their details, and when you have a clear idea of how the drawing board is made and put together, then sit

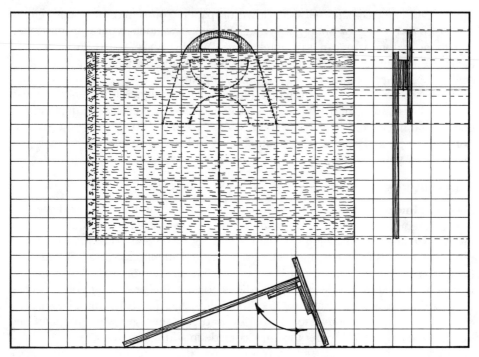

11-1 Working Drawing #1. (top) Front, end, and open-section views. The scale is 1 grid square to 1 inch.

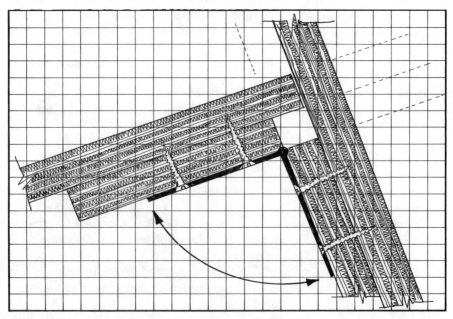

11-2 Working Drawing #2. Section detail of the hinge mechanism. The scale is 4 grid squares to 1 inch.

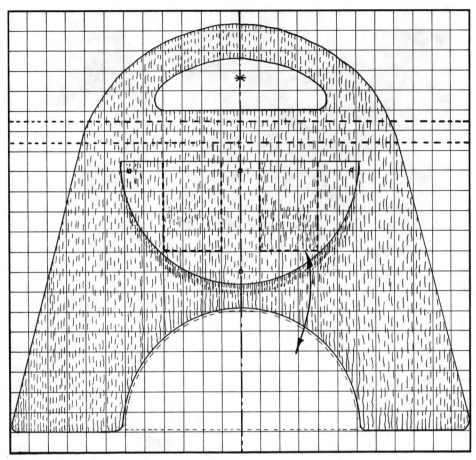

11-3 Working Drawing #3. Note the half-circle hinge-plate and the various alignment guides of the handle-stand. The scale is 2 grid squares to 1 inch.

down with the pencil, ruler, and workout paper and finalize the design. Draw the A handle-stand up to full size and make a good tracing.

3. Set the ½-inch-thick 48-x-24-inch sheet of plywood flat-down on the clean worksurface, and use the pencil, ruler, and T-square to set out the 28-x-20-inch drawing board. Make sure that your measurements are accurate, and see to it that all the right angles are square and true (FIG. 11-5).

4. When you are happy that all is correct, take the crosscut saw and first cut the sheet down into two manageable pieces, and then cut the drawing surface to size. Use a straight-sided length of scrap wood clamped to the work as a saw guide (FIG. 11-6). When you have achieved the 28-x-20 board, set it best-face-up on the worksurface, lightly pencil label the edges TOP, BOTTOM, LEFT, and RIGHT, and then put it to one side.

5. Take the 24-inch-long metal ruler and mark it off at the 20-inch mark so that it fits along the LEFT edge of the drawing board. This done, set it in the jaws

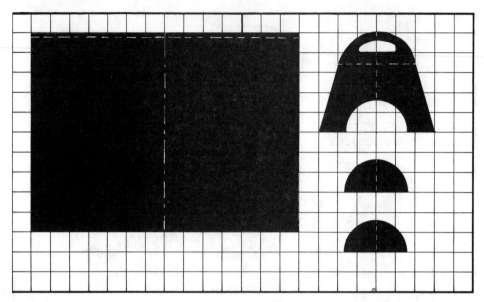

11-4 Design template. The four component cutouts that make up the project—the board, the handle/stand, and the two hinge-plates. The scale is 1 grid square to 2 inches.

11-5 Use the pencil ruler and T-square to set out the drawing board.

of a muffled vice and use the hacksaw to cut it to length. Set the ruler between two pieces of wood and secure it in so that the cut end is uppermost. Run the file across and along the cut edge until it is smooth and free from burrs (FIG. 11-7, top).

6. Run a pencil centerline down the best face of the ruler, and then strike it off ½ inch in from each end, and at the 5-inch, 10-inch, and 15-inch marks. Use the hammer and centerpunch to set each of these marks in with a dent.

7. With the ruler supported on a length of scrap wood and clamped firm-down

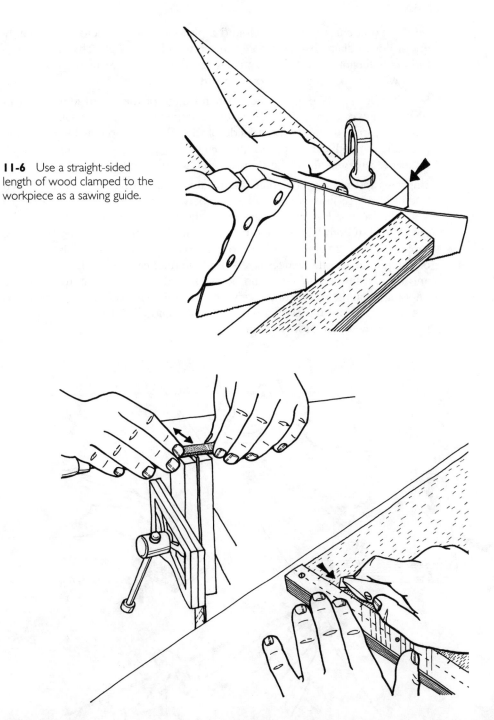

11-6 Use a straight-sided length of wood clamped to the workpiece as a sawing guide.

11-7 (left) Clamp the ruler between two pieces of scrap wood and use the file to remove all sharp edges and burrs. (right) Tack the ruler in place with a couple of screws, then score along the board-side of the ruler so as to cut down into the wood to the thickness of the ruler.

on the workbench, take the drill and a bit to match your screws—probably about ⅛ inch diameter—and bore the screw holes through. This done, carefully countersink each hole so that when the screws are in place they are flush with or even slightly below the surface.

8. Set the ruler in place along the left-hand edge of the board and tack it in place with two screws. Having carefully checked the alignment, take the craft knife and score along the board-side of the ruler so as to cut down into the plywood to the thickness of the ruler. Figure on about two thicknesses of the multicore as being about the right depth (FIG. 11-7, bottom).

9. Unscrew and remove the ruler. Clamp the board firm-down on the bench (Don't forget to have a piece of scrap between the board and the clamp.) With the bevel-edge chisel, pare away the ruler width of waste. With the chisel held in both hands—one pushing and the other controlling (FIG. 11-8, top)—and, being very careful not to cut too deep or to let the chisel run out of control, remove the veneer layers until the ruler can be bedded down level and flush with the surface of the board. Spend time getting it just right; it's important that the ruler-fixing screws are flush. Use a block and sandpaper to rub the edges and the face down to a good, smooth finish. Work in the direction of the grain (FIG. 11-8, right).

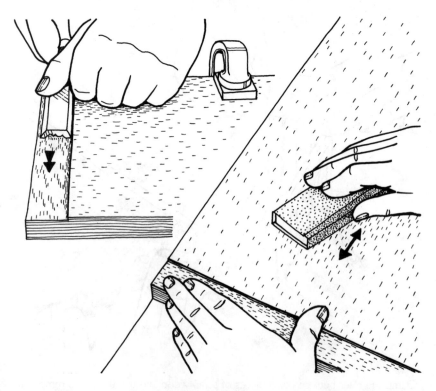

11-8 Clamp the board to the workbench and carefully pare and lower the wood. Use the block and sandpaper to rub the wood down to a smooth-to-the-touch finish.

10. When you have lowered the waste and rubbed down to a good finish, clear the bench clutter and carefully screw-fit the ruler in place.

11. Having had a good look at the drawing (FIG. 11-3) and drawn the handle-stand to size, make a good tracing, pencil-press transfer the traced lines through to the remaining piece of plywood. This done, remove the tracing and use the pencil, ruler, and compass to establish the shape of the handle. Draw out the half-circle hinge-plates, draw in the centerlines and so on.

    Note that as the two hinge-plates and the between leg half-circle, are all compass-drawn to a diameter of 6 inches, you could (if you were careful) use the half-circle of waste—the bit from the bottom of the stand—as one of the hinge-plates. Drill out the pilot/starter hole in the handle waste area (see asterisk FIG. 11-3).

12. Having drilled a saw blade starter hole through the area of handle waste, secure the workpiece in the vice and use the coping saw to fret out the shapes. The outside profiles are easy enough—you just run the saw blade a little to the waste side of the drawn line, making sure that you hold the saw so that the blade is at right angles to the working face, and keep repositioning the workpiece so that the blade is always presented with the line of next cut.

13. When you are ready to cut out the window of inside-handle waste, unhitch the saw blade. Pass the blade through the pilot hole (FIG. 11-9), refit and retension the blade, and then continue to cut as already described. Sand the parts to a good finish.

14. Clear the workbench and sweep it clean, then take the four components—the board, the handle-stand, and the two half-circle hinge-plates—and use the pencil and ruler to re-establish the various centerlines and guidelines. Each half-circle needs a centerline, the handle-stand needs a top-to-bottom centerline and a side-to-side guideline that is set parallel and 6¾ inch up from

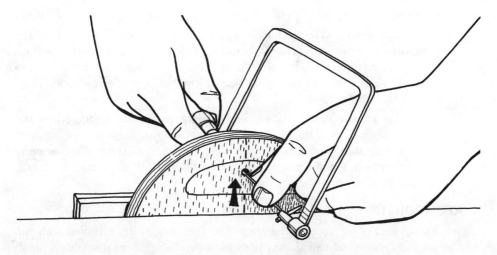

11-9 (top) Work on the waste side of the drawn line to cut away the shape.

the baseline, and the back of the drawing board needs a top-to-bottom centerline and a guideline that is ½ inch down from the top edge (FIG. 11-3).

15. With the handle-stand set down on the workbench so that the guidelines are uppermost, pin and glue-fix one half-circle hinge-plate in place so that its straight edge is 6¾ inches up from the baseline, and so that all centerlines are aligned (FIG. 11-10). Repeat this procedure with the drawing board and the other hinge-plate, only this time, of course, have the straight edge of the hinge-plate set ½ inch down from the back top edge of the board.

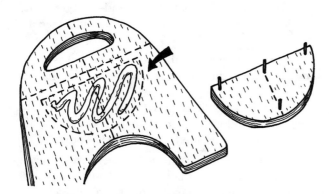

11-10 Making sure the centerlines and guides are carefully aligned, glue and pin the half-circle hinge-plate in place.

16. When the glue is dry, set the handle-stand down on the bench so that the hinge-plate is uppermost, and screw-fix the two hinges in position. With the hinges set about ½ inch either side of the centerline, the fixing procedure is:
    • Pencil mark the position of the hinges.
    • Hold the hinge in place and spike one screw hole with the bradawl (FIG. 11-11, left).
    • Fit one screw, spike the other holes, and fit the other screws.

17. With the hinges fitted to the handle-stand, spread a protective cloth over the worksurface, clamp the drawing board face-down so the top edge is flush with the edge of the bench, hold the handle-stand in place so that all centerlines are aligned and fit the other sides of the hinges as already described (FIG. 11-11, right).

18. When you are happy that all is fitted correctly, check that all the edges and surfaces are smooth to the touch, wipe away the dust, and—not forgetting to give the varnish a swift rubdown between dry coats—lay on three or more coats of varnish. Finally, put your name on the back of the board. Your customized drafting unit is ready for use.

WATCHPOINTS

If you like the idea of the project, but are not so keen on getting involved with cutting metal, then you could use an acrylic or hardwood strip as an inset edge, rather than a metal ruler.

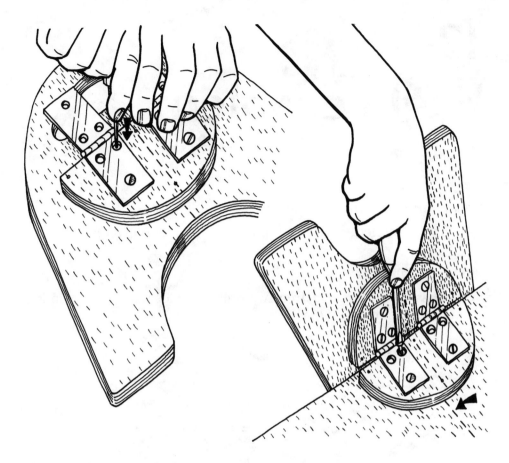

11-11 (top) Use the bradawl to make starter holes for the screws. (bottom) Clamp the board face-down on a cloth-muffled bench, align the handle/stand with the various guidelines, and screw the hinges to the other half-circle plate.

If you don't want to go to the trouble of insetting the ruler, you could screw-fix the ruler directly to the face of the board, and then use a stick-on plastic sheet to bring the rest of the board to the level of the ruler.

If you want to go for an ultra-lightweight board, you could fit a single plastic/nylon carbon fiber hinge.

You could have rubber foot studs/tips to prevent the board slipping.

For easy storage, you could design a special wall hook/bracket.

12
Eagle emblem

Making an American eagle letter rack:

A mantel shelf letter rack with patriotic American imagery.

Primary techniques:

Compass work, using a fretsaw, drilling holes, sanding, painting, and careful putting together.

Age level: 14–15

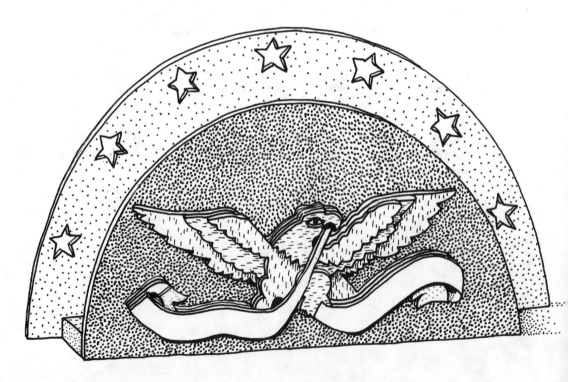

WOODS

A sheet of best-quality ¼-inch-thick birch-faced multicore plywood at 12½ × 12½ inches for the two half-circles. This allows for a small amount of cutting waste.

A sheet of best-quality ⅛-inch-thick birch-faced multicore plywood at 12 × 12 inches -for the five layers that make up the eagle. This allows for a generous amount of cutting waste.

A 12-inch length of prepared, straight-grained wood, such as beech or pine, at ½ inch thick and about 2¼ inches wide—for the base.

TOOLS AND MATERIALS

- Fretsaw and a pack of spare blades
- Bird's mouth cutting board with a clamp to fit (to be used with the fretsaw)
- Workout and tracing paper
- Pencil and ruler
- Compass and try square
- Small hand drill with bits to fit
- Small clamp
- Small tenon or gents brass-backed saw
- Bench hook
- Loctite Super Glue 3
- A handful of ¾-inch-long brass pins or brads
- Small pin or peen hammer.
- Package of medium- to fine-grade sandpaper
- Acrylic paints in red, white, and blue
- Clear, high-shine varnish
- Two paintbrushes, a broad and a fine-point

KIDS'-EYE VIEW

Just imagine: It's mid-morning and you are lazing in bed. Your dad has slaved away in the kitchen and brought you up a full breakfast—two eggs, crisp bacon, toast, and sausages. Your mother is doing your homework and ironing your socks, and your kid brothers and sisters are quietly standing by—just in case you should want another cup of coffee. Suddenly you hear the flip-flap of the mailbox. Your dad runs downstairs and brings up a stack of letters. Great! Huge checks from adoring relations, letters from a beau, letters from a steady, letters from a secret admirer, letters from a hero-worshiper, letters from lovesick fans. But where to put all your letters? Well, no problem—with our all-American rack, you can slot the mail in order and get your social secretary to answer it at a later date. Ha—what a dream! Still . . . the letter rack is a good idea!

CAREGIVERS' GUIDE

Making Time and Skill Level—This is one of those projects where although the woodworking techniques are relatively basic—the measuring out and the fretsawing—the final putting together, painting, and the arranging are somewhat finger-twisting. I think it fair to say that if the paintwork is slap-dash, the layered cutouts out of alignment, and the sanding less than perfect, then the project will be a mess-up. That said, I would say that a careful, painstaking 14- to 15-year-old kid who enjoys working slowly at his/her own pace, should be able to have this project made in a couple of easy weekends.

Cautions and Adult Help—No problems with this project, a 14–15 year old should be able to manage without help. Okay—so you might well offer a few tips, like . . . spend a lot of pre-project time working it out with card and scissors, and . . . don't rush the fretsawing, and . . . make a good job of the sanding, and so on, but really, a keen teenager ought to be able to figure it out.

The good news is, you need have no worries about safety. The fretwork is just about as safe, as safe can be! A swift talk-over with the kids, and then you can make something of your own, while they get on with it.

GETTING DOWN TO WORK

1. Have a look at the project picture (page 130), the working drawings (FIGS. 12-1 and 12-2) and see how the project is made up from eight primary wooden components—the 12-inch-diameter backboard, the 10-inch-diameter front-board, the 2¼-inch-wide, 10-inch-long base, and the five ⅛-inch-thick layers that make up the eagle emblem. See how, from the back layer through to the front, the various eagle profiles have been successively cut back to create the illusion that the bird and the banner have rounded depth. Generally run your eyes backwards and forwards over the details—the pierced stars in the back-board, the simple construction, the use of flat primary colors, and so on—until you have a clear understanding of what needs to go where and how.

2. Set the 12½-x-12½-inch sheet of ¼-inch-thick plywood flat-down on the work-bench, establish its center by drawing crossed diagonals, and then run a side-to-side line across the board to divide it into two halves.

3. Now, one half of the board at a time, first set the compass to a radius of 6 inches and strike off a 12-inch-diameter half-circle. Then set the compass to a radius of 5 inches and strike off a 10-inch-diameter half-circle. When you have drawn out the two half-circles, reset the compass to 5½ inches, and go back to the 12-inch-diameter half-circle and set out a centerline for the stars (FIG. 12-3). When you have double-checked that all is correct, use the tenon saw to cut the two half-circles apart.

4. With the two half-circles carefully set out, clamp the bird's mouth cutting board to the edge of the workbench and set to work with the fretsaw. The order of work is:

   • Clamp the bird's mouth board in place.
   • Set the blade in the fretsaw frame so that the teeth are pointing down towards the handle, and adjust the tension so that the blade is taut.

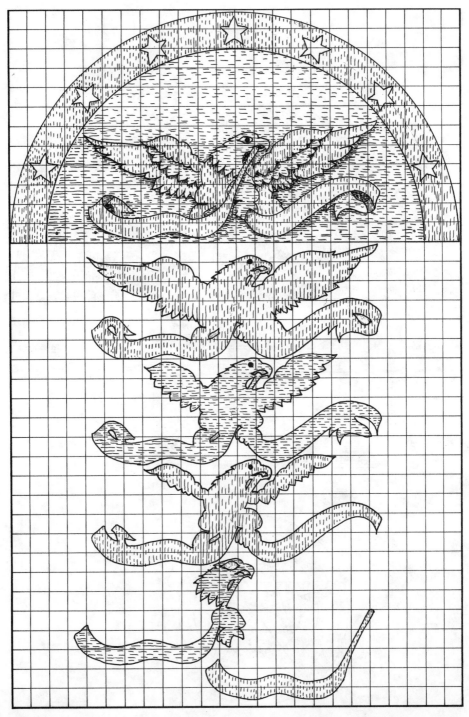

12-1 Working Drawing. The scale is 2 grid squares to 1 inch. Note that the eagle is made up from five layers.

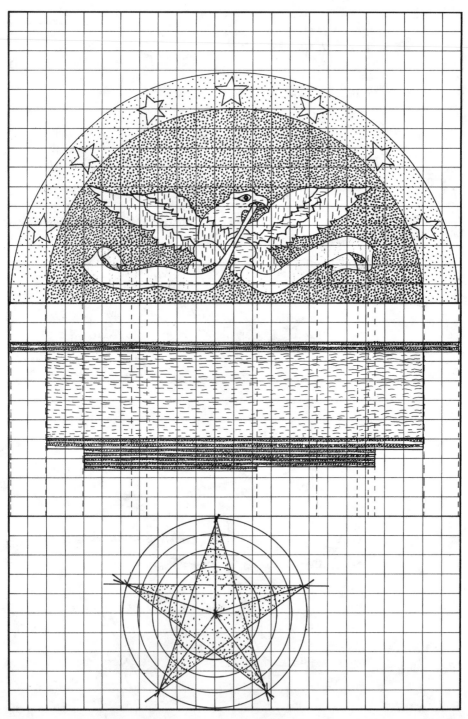

12-2 Painting Grid and Working Drawing. (top) The scale is 2 grid squares to 1 inch. (bottom) The five-point star is not to scale.

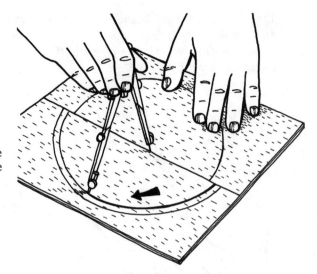

12-3 Reset the compass to a radius of 5½ inches, go back to the 12-inch-diameter half-circle and set out a centerline for the arc of stars.

- Hold the wood firm-down on the cutting board and enter the blade a little to the waste side of the drawn line.
- Work at a steady, easy pace, all the while moving the workpiece so that the saw is presented with the line of best cut, and holding the saw so that the cut line runs through the thickness at right angles to the working face (FIG. 12-4).

Continue cutting carefully around one half-circle curve and then the other, until both boards have been worked.

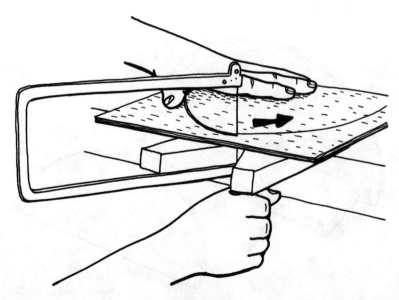

12-4 Hold the saw so that the cut line runs through the wood at right angles to the working face.

5. Take the 12-inch-long 2¼-inch-wide piece of wood—the piece for the base—and use the pencil, ruler, and try square to set out the 10-inch length. This done, brace the wood hard up against the bench hook and use the tenon saw to cut it to length (FIG. 12-5).

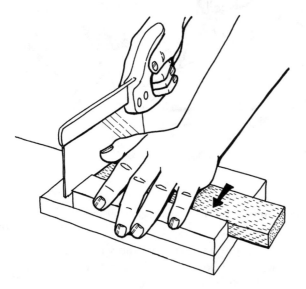

12-5 Hold the wood hard up against the bench hook and use the tenon saw to cut the wood to length.

6. Now, take the three components—the two half-circles and the base—and have a trial dry-run put-together (FIG. 12-6). When you are happy with the fit and size, take the graded sandpaper and rub all cut edges and faces down to a smooth finish.

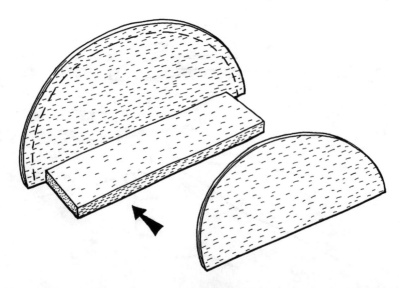

12-6 Have a trial put-together of the two half-circles and the base; check and adjust for a good fit.

7. Study the design template for the eagle (FIG. 12-7) and draw the eagle up to full size. Carefully trace off the five profiles that make up the total eagle, then pencil-press transfer the five profiles through to the ⅛-inch-thick plywood. Bear in mind that shared profile lines, such as the scroll, the head, and the beak, need to be well matched, so spend time setting them out with extra care.

   Note: you can vary the direction of the grain for the various layers (FIG. 12-1).

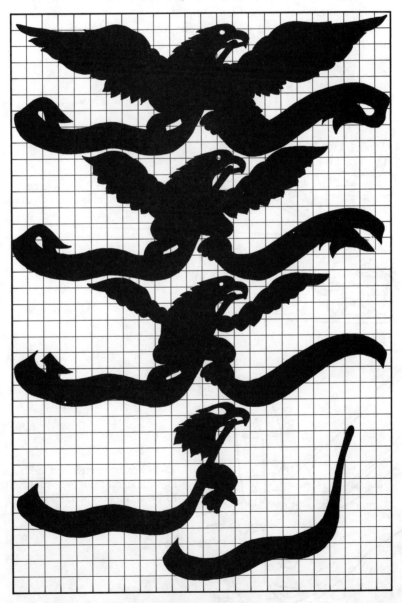

12-7 Design Template. The scale is 3 grid squares to 1 inch.

8. When you are happy with the way the five profiles are set out, go back to the saw table and repeat the fretsawing procedure as already described. Take it nice and easy, all the while trying to run the line of cut a little to the waste side of the drawn line.

To cut out an enclosed area of waste (such as the end of scroll or the outer eye) first drill a ⅟₁₆-inch-diameter pilot hole through the waste area (FIG. 12-8). Then return to the bird's mouth cutting board, unhitch the blade, pass one end through the pilot hole, refit and retension the blade, and continue cutting as already described (FIG. 12-9).

Note: Be very careful when you are cutting the delicate beak areas; make sure that all beaks match.

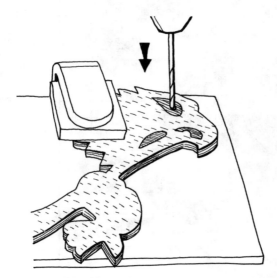

12-8 Use the ⅟₁₆-inch-diameter drill bit to bore pilot holes through all the enclosed areas of waste.

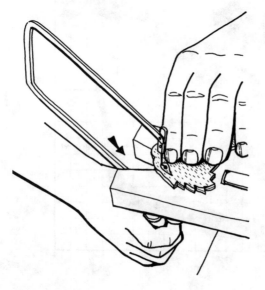

12-9 Having retensioned the blade in the saw frame, cut from the pilot hole through to the waste side of the drawn line.

9. Take the backboard—the largest of the two half-circles—and use the try square to run a line straight up from what was the circle center, and on through to the circumference. Now, taking the point where this line crosses the center-of-star arc as being 12 o'clock high, set the compass to a radius of 2 inches, and work out from 12 o'clock high striking off 2-inch step-offs. With one star at top center and three at either side, there should be a total of seven stars in all.

10. Trace off the five-point star motif (FIG. 12-2) and carefully pencil-press transfer the images through to the backboard. Have the stars aligned so that the centers are set on the 2-inch step-off points, and so that one point of the star is looking towards the edge and away from the center of the half-circle.

11. Run a single ⅛-inch-diameter drill hole through the center of each star (FIG. 12-10), and cut out the little star-shaped window of waste as already described. While you have the drill to hand, bore eye holes through the three primary eagle cutouts—meaning the three at the back.

12. When all the components have been cut to shape and size and have been variously drilled, pierced, and fitted, rub all faces and cut edges down with the fine-grade sandpaper until they are smooth to the touch.

    Special Tip: When you come to some of the small, difficult-to-get-at-areas, wrap a scrap of sandpaper around a stick and use it like a file.

13. Having wiped off all the dust and moved to the clean dust-free area that you have prepared for painting, mix the paints and set out the four components that need to be painted—the star-spangled backboard to be painted blue, the

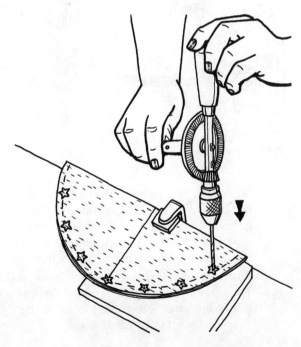

12-10 With the workpiece clamped down over a scrap of waste wood, bore ⅛-inch-diameter holes through each of the stars.

front board to be painted red, and the two banner pieces to be painted white. See painting grid (FIG. 12-2).

14. Start by giving the two half-circle boards a couple of all-over coats of paint—one blue and the other red. Carefully paint all faces and edges. This done, take the fine-point paintbrush and the white paint and paint the banner. The single from-the-beak half-banner piece is easy enough—just paint the front face and the edges. The from-the-claw half-banner is a little more difficult in that you have to paint the banner so that the paint line will be covered by the head-claw profile.

15. When the paint is dry, then comes the pleasuresome task of putting the project together. Start by gluing and sandwiching up the layers that make the eagle. With the back profile set down on the worksurface, one layer at a time, dribble the Super Glue on mating surfaces, and carefully place the profiles together. Make sure that all profile edges are correctly aligned especially the wing edges and the head (FIG. 12-11).

16. Pencil-mark areas to be glued, swiftly rub through the paint on mating surfaces, and glue and pin-fix the two half-circles one either side of the base block (FIG. 12-12).

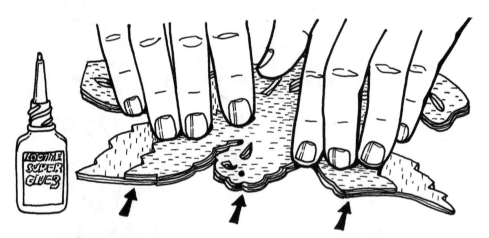

12-11 Position the layers so that the wing and head edges are carefully aligned.

17. When you are happy with the fit of the two half-circles, and again having pencil marked and rubbed through the paint on mating surfaces, dribble a generous amount of Super Glue over the back of the eagle emblem and set it down in place on the red painted half-circle. Bed it down firmly by applying pressure and moving it slightly from side to side.

18. When the glue is dry, inspect the piece and trim excess glue with the knife. Then take the white paint and the fine-point brush and carefully paint in the rest of the banner, the little pieces on the end, and the edges and any other areas that need to be made good.

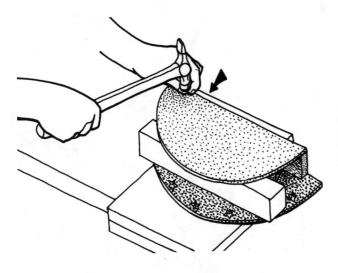

12-12 Brace the components up against the bench hook and support the top half-circle with a block of scrap wood.

19. Finally, when the paint is completely dry, give the whole project a couple of coats of clear, high-shine varnish, carefully brush away dribbles and build-up, and the letter rack is ready for its place on the mantel shelf.

WATCHPOINTS

If you can get to use an electric scroll saw, you can speed up the project by setting five pieces of ply together and cutting the eagle out all at one time. Once you have cut out five identical profiles, you could trim back each one to fit the design. Working in this way it is possible to achieve a perfect alignment of the edges.

If you like the design but want to go for a more lavish paint job, you could paint the eagle gold, and maybe even build stars-and-stripes imagery into the backboard design.

The plain white banner allows space for customizing the work—a short name, a message, a date, initials, or whatever.

13
Pretty precious

Making laminated jewelry:

Delicate jewelry made by laminating, sanding, sawing, rearranging, and slicing solid wood and veneers.

Primary techniques:

Using a brass-backed gents saw, gluing, laminating, sanding, slicing, and putting together.

Age level: 14–15

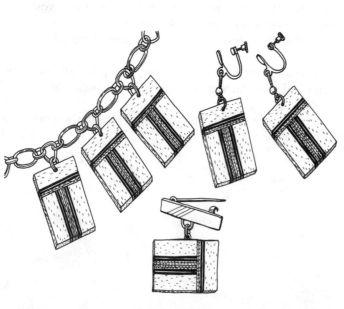

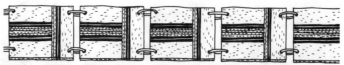

WOODS

- A 12-inch length of prepared, best-quality white/pink hard-textured wood at ¼ inch thick and ⅞ inch wide. You could use boxwood, yew, pear, or whatever, as long as it's hard-textured, straight-grained, white/pink in color, completely free from knots and stains, and with the grain running across the width of the strip.
- Two 12-inch lengths of dyed black sycamore veneer at about ¹⁄₃₂ inch thick and ⅞ inch wide, with the grain running across the width.
  Note: If you can get a single length at ¹⁄₁₆ inch thick, then so much the better.
- Two 12-inch lengths of dyed turquoise sycamore veneer at about ¹⁄₃₂ inch thick and ⅞ inch wide, with the grain running across the width.
  Note: Just as with the black veneer, if you can get a thicker veneer at about ¹⁄₁₆ inch, then all the better.

The veneer thickness isn't crucial. We use two ¹⁄₃₂-inch thicknesses sandwiched together—two black and two turquoise—but you could better use single thicknesses at about ¹⁄₁₆ to ³⁄₃₂ inch. It is important with the boxwood and the veneers that the grain runs across the width of the strips.

TOOLS AND MATERIALS

- Small, fine-bladed brass-backed gents saw
- Small G-clamps
- Boards to be used with the clamps
- Pencil and ruler
- Sandpaper, medium-fine and fine
- A couple of sheets of ½-inch-thick plywood to fit the size of the sandpaper
- Quick-dry glue or contact adhesive
- Cascamite resin woodworking glue
- Two-tube pack of resin glue
- Bench with vice
- Bench hook
- Small hand drill with bits to fit
- A pack of white metal/silver jewelry findings to suit the design of the piece of jewelry that you have in mind.
- Clear, high-shine polyurethane varnish
- Small fine-point brush
- Cord line knotted at 2-inch intervals
- Paper clips

Note about jewelry findings: You could have little hooks or screw-on fittings for pierced earrings, links for a chain, cuff-link clips, badge pins, tie clips, and so on. Send to a jewelry supplier for a list and see what they have to offer.

KIDS'-EYE VIEW

Earrings, bangles, bracelets, necklaces, medallions, broaches, key fobs, cuff-links, and badges all say something about the way we see ourselves. Jewelry makes us feel beautiful, handsome, strong, well-dressed, street-wise, and so on; jewelry makes us feel special.

When I was a kid—I must have been about 12 years old—my brother and I used to dress up in old clothes and have a wild time. One moment we were pirates, and then Indians, and then South Sea islanders, and so on. It didn't matter to us what characters we were supposed to be. We just liked dressing up and wearing our granny's costume jewelry.

Okay . . . so you can imagine the look on my dad's face when he saw his two sons decked out in beads, bangles, and old fur coats! But then how could he know that we thought of ourselves as wild, macho mountain men?—lots of bear claws, beads, feathers, gold chains, magic amulets, and long hair. You know the sort of thing, a sort of cross between Davy Crockett and an Indian Shaman.

If you want to make some jewelry for yourself, or for your mom or dad, or for your aunt or a special friend, then this is the project for you.

CAREGIVERS' GUIDE

Making Time and Skill Level—This is one of those projects that is not so much difficult as finicky. The tools are small, the pieces of wood are small, and the working methods require lots of small, tight, delicate procedures. But then again, lots of kids particularly enjoy working on a small, painstaking scale.

As to what type of jewelry you and the kids decide to make from the basic repeat-slice components, they can be built up into earrings and necklaces, belts, broaches and charms, or just about anything that takes your fancy. Start by making contact with a craft supplier and getting a findings catalog (meaning a lists that describes all the little chains, links, clips, and fixing that you need to make jewelry). Most findings are fixed with small metal rings called *jump rings*, so you will probably need a couple of pairs of long-nosed pliers.

Although a well motivated 14- to 15-year-old should be able to get the component slices made in a weekend, the actual putting together to make the jewelry—waiting for the glue to dry, building the components, and so on—will take longer. Best to think of this project as a way of making a stockpile of components—like beads or semiprecious stones—that can be used at a later stage.

Cautions and Adult Help—If you or the kids can't quite visualize how this project is made, have a pre-project workout with a few slices of colored modeling clay and/or glue and colored cardboard. Although technically this is a pretty straightforward project, children might need some help and encouragement when it comes to the sanding.

Be Warned—Fine wood dust can be allergenic and generally can make your eyes run and water. Either do the sanding out in the garden, or at the very least, stop every few minutes and clear up the dust with a vacuum cleaner. If you are worried, wear masks.

GETTING DOWN TO WORK

1. Have a close-up look at the project picture (page 142) and the working drawings (FIG. 13-1), and see how the jewelry has been laminated, cut, rearranged, and sliced. Note how the initial 12-inch-long laminate is made from a single ¼-x-⅞-inch section of boxwood plus two colored veneers, which is in turn cut into three 4-inch lengths and then further laminated to make the primary ready-to-slice stock.

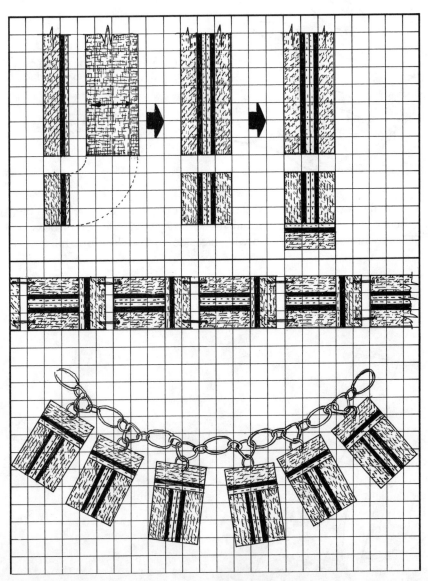

13-1 Working Drawing. The scale is 4 grid squares to 1 inch. (top left) First lamination.(top middle) Second lamination. (top right) Third lamination. (bottom) Jewelry ideas.

2. Bearing in mind that at just about every stage you need to do a lot of sanding, start by using the quick-set contact adhesive to fix the sheets of sandpaper grit-side-up onto the two sheets of ½-inch plywood, so as to make two nice and level sanding boards (FIG. 13-2).

13-2 Making a sanding board by mounting the sandpaper onto a sheet of plywood.

3. Take the two sanding boards and screw or pin them grit-side-up on the workbench. This done, take the ¼-inch-thick, ⅞-inch-wide length of boxwood and swiftly rub one of the ⅞-inch-wide faces down to a clean true finish (FIG. 13-3).

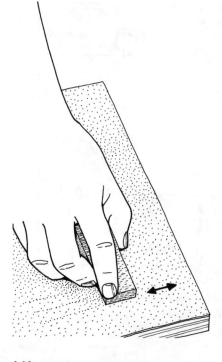

13-3 Rub one of the ⅞-inch-wide faces down to a clean, true finish.

4. Take the two G-clamps (or a press), the two clamping boards, a couple of sheets of newspaper, the wood, and the veneers, and have a trial clamp-up. From left to right, the clamping order is: clamping board, newspaper, boxwood, black veneers, turquoise veneers, newspaper, and then the final clamping board. Decide in your own mind just what goes where and how (FIG. 13-4).

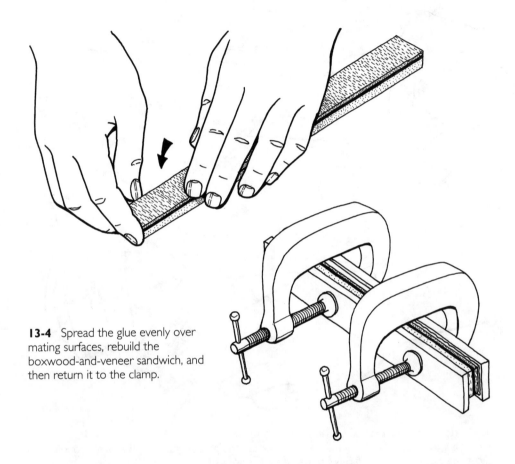

13-4 Spread the glue evenly over mating surfaces, rebuild the boxwood-and-veneer sandwich, and then return it to the clamp.

5. When you are happy with the arrangement, smear the Cascamite resin glue on all mating surfaces of the little boxwood and veneer sandwich, check that everything is aligned, and then clamp-up.

6. When the glue is dry, unscrew the clamp, carefully remove the glued-up sandwich, and put the clamps and boards to one side.

7. Now, having used the pencil, ruler, and try-square to carefully divide the sandwich into three equal 4-inch lengths, butt the workpiece hard up against the bench hook, and use the gents saw to cut it down into three lengths (FIG. 13-5, top). Take two of the lengths, wipe away any wood dust, smear Cascamite glue on the turquoise faces, set them carefully together face-to-

face so that the turquoise veneers are touching (FIG. 13-5, bottom), and then clamp up as already described.

8. When the glue is dry, remove the wood from the clamp and then sand both the long, multicolored, edge-of-wood faces down to a smooth level finish (FIG. 13-6).

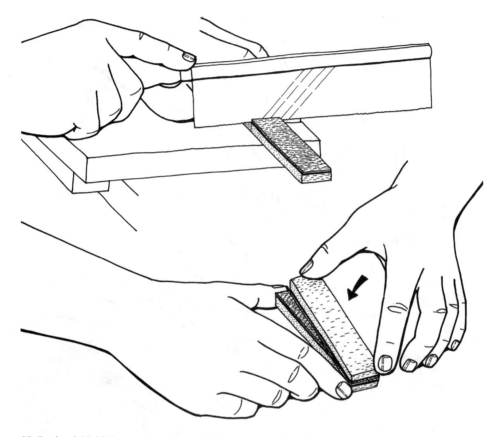

13-5 (top) Hold the marked-up sandwich hard up against the bench hook and use the gents saw to cut it into three 4-inch lengths. (bottom) Spread the glue evenly over the two turquoise surfaces and set them face-to-face with the side edges aligned.

9. Having again wiped up all the wood dust, smear glue on one of the long, multicolored faces, then set the third 4-inch length turquoise-face-down on the glue. Check that all is correct and then clamp up as already described (FIG. 13-7).

10. When the glue is completely dry, remove the wood from the clamps and clear the worksurface of all clutter.

11. Now take your 4-inch glued-up block, and set to work carefully rubbing all six faces down to a smooth finish.

12. When you have achieved a clean-cut laminated block, secure the bench hook

13-6 Sand all the long multistriped edge-of-wood faces to a smooth level finish.

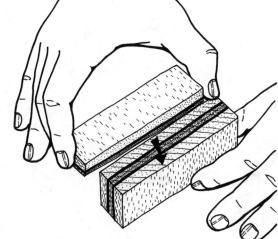

13-7 Spread the glue evenly on one striped mating face, take the single 4-inch length, set the turquoise-face down on the glued face, and clamp up.

in the vice, set the block hard up against the stop, and use the gents saw to cut the wood down into as many ⅛-inch-thick end-of-block slices as possible. The order of work should go: Use a pencil, ruler, and square to set out a ⅛-inch-thick slice; cut the slice off with the saw; and so on.

Allowing for saw cut or kerf waste between slices, you should finish up with 20 or so slices (FIG. 13-8).

13. If your chosen piece of jewelry requires that the laminated slices are pierced—for chain links or earring fixings—set the appropriate diameter bit in the drill, carefully establish the number and position of the holes, secure the slice in a little scrap-wood-and-pins jig, and then bore them through (FIG. 13-9).

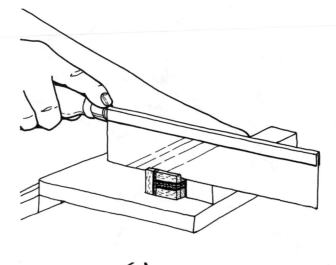

13-8 Use the gents saw to cut off ⅛-inch-thick end-of-block slices.

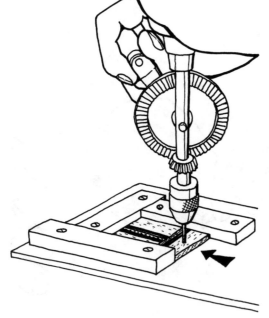

13-9 Having made a little jig with a few scraps of wood—pinned or screwed to a board/bench—hold the workpiece secure and drill the fixing holes.

14. With the holes drilled, take the slices one at a time and systematically rub them down on the sanding boards—first on the medium and then on the fine grade—until all the faces and edges are silky-smooth to the touch.

15. Wipe away all the dust, clean up the debris, and move to the dust-free area that you have set aside for varnishing. Rig up the knotted cord line, bend the paper clips to make one hook for each of the laminated slices, and generally make ready for varnishing.

    Special Tip: The knots on the line prevent the varnish pieces from sliding along and touching.

16. When you are happy with the arrangement, give each slice a coat of clear varnish, then hang them up to dry. Sand slightly and re-varnish. Repeat this procedure three or four times until the slices are a high-shine finish. *Note:* You might need to clear the varnish from the holes.

17. Finally, when the laminated slices are completely dry, use the findings to achieve the desired jewelry.

WATCHPOINTS

If you like the idea of the project, but have in mind to make a lot of jewelry, then start off with longer strips of wood.

A band saw would certainly speed up the whole project, but then again, cutting small pieces of wood on a band saw is potentially very dangerous. An experienced woodworking adult would need to watch over the whole procedure.

Be warned: It is important that you use a hard resin glue like Cascamite, rather than PVA. If you do use PVA, the rubbery structure of the glue will quickly make a mess-up of the sanding boards and might even smear across the surface of the laminated slices.

14
Pocket puzzle

Making a Japanese puzzle cross:

A small hand-sized puzzle made from notched and pierced wood.

Primary techniques:

Compass work, using a small brass-backed saw, using a coping saw, chisel work, sanding, staining, and waxing.

Age level: 14–15

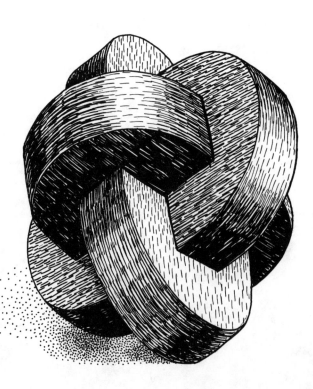

WOOD

- A sheet of best-quality ½-inch-thick birch-faced multicore plywood at 2 inches wide and 10 inches long. This allows a small amount for cutting waste.

TOOLS AND MATERIALS

- Coping saw and blades
- Gents brass-backed saw, or small tenon saw
- Workbench with vice
- Workout paper
- Pencil and ruler
- Compass
- Marking gauge
- Try square
- Small strap-steel clamp
- Bevel-edge chisel, ¼ inch or ³⁄₁₆ inch wide
- Small hand drill with ³⁄₁₆-inch-diameter bit
- Graded sandpaper
- Large felt-tip, black, spirit marker pen
- Wax furniture polish
- Fluff-free polishing cloth

KIDS'-EYE VIEW

Most of us enjoy playing around with puzzles! Jigsaws, wire-link brain-teasers, wooden block puzzles, plastic twist-and-push cube puzzles, and animals that come apart—they are all good fun. But best of all, I think, are the small, traditional, hold-in-the-hand wooden push-and-slide puzzles.

Puzzles are just perfect for all those boring stand-around-and-wait moments. I'm sure you know what I mean—waiting for the school bus, for a meal, for your friends to turn up, and so on. At such moments, you can take the puzzle out of your pocket or bag, and while away the time taking it apart and putting it back together. And, of course, when you have mastered the puzzle, you can give it to a friend or your mom or dad and have fun watching them try to figure it out. (Don't forget to tell your dad, though, that brute-force King-Kong tactics aren't allowed—no twisting, wrenching, bending, or biting!)

A puzzle that is skill-stretchingly tricky to make, and then just as tricky to put together once it has been made, has got to be a GREAT idea! Are you ready for the challenge?

CAREGIVERS' GUIDE

Making Time and Skill Level—Although, on the face of it, the puzzle looks so easy that it is hardly worth the bother, it is actually a project that calls for a deal of careful measuring and tool work. This is not to say that you need to be a woodworking guru or own a huge tool kit, but rather that the success of the project hinges on your being able to measure-mark-and-cut with quiet care and precision. I would say that the average 14- to 15-year-old should be able to have this project made in a weekend.

Cautions and Adult Help—While a 14- to 15-year-old should be able to manage this project on his/her own, why don't you all have a go? You could see who could make the best-fitting puzzle, or you could each try using a different wood or decorative technique. There are any number of exciting possibilities. It could be really good fun.

GETTING DOWN TO WORK

1. Have a good long look at the project picture (page 152) and the working drawings (FIG. 14-1), and consider how the puzzle is made up from three identical, curve-ended profiles. See also how, at a scale of 4 grid squares to 1 inch, the three link-like components each measure 2½ inches long, 1½ inches wide, and ½ inch thick. Note how important it is that the primary central slot be ½ inch wide to fit the thickness of the ply, and 1½ inches long to fit the 1½-inch width of the link.

2. When you have a clear understanding of how the project needs to be made and put together, take the pencil, ruler, compass, and square and draw the three components out to full size on the workout paper. You might have to do this a couple of times before you understand just how the various slots relate to each other.

3. Having ironed out all the problems by drawing the forms out on the workout paper, draw the three primary 2½-x-1½-inch rectangles out end-to-end on the plywood so that they make a strip 1½ inches wide and 10 inches long. The 10 inches allows for a generous amount of cutting waste between each component.

4. Take the small tenon saw, set the workpiece in the vice, and cut away the edge waste on the waste side of the drawn line so that you have a strip that is a fraction oversize in width (FIG. 14-2).

5. When you have achieved the 10-inch-long strip, take the sandpaper, pin it grit-side-up to a plywood board, and then set to work rubbing the sides of the strip down to a smooth, crisp, clean-edged 1½-inch-width finish (FIG. 14-3.)

6. With the pencil, ruler, try square, and marking gauge, set out all the measurements that make up the design. Draw in the centerline, set the gauge to ½ inch, and strike off the central slot. Set the compass to a radius of ¾ inch and draw out the 1½-inch-wide end half-circles. You should now have three identical curve-end shapes drawn out along the strip (FIG. 14-4)

7. When you are happy with the arrangement, set the wood in the vice and use the coping saw first to swiftly cut the strip down into the three manageable pieces and then to cut out the three curve-ended components. Be sure to run

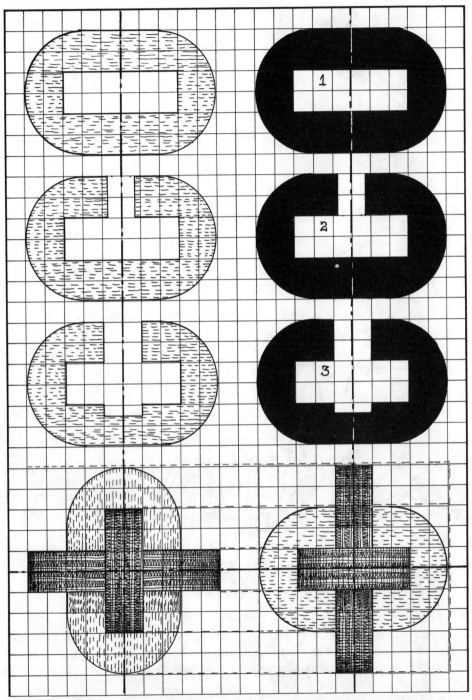

14-1 Working Drawing. At a scale of 4 grid squares to 1 inch, each of the three small, round-ended components measures 2½ inches long, 1½ inches wide and ½ inch thick. Note how the three components are numbered 1, 2, and 3.

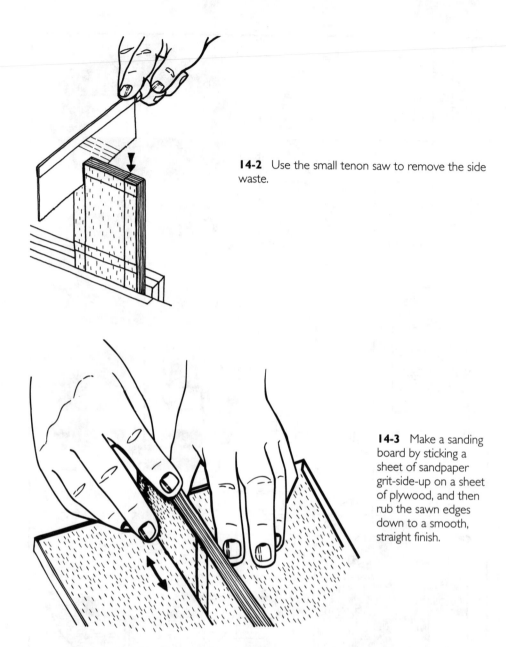

14-2 Use the small tenon saw to remove the side waste.

14-3 Make a sanding board by sticking a sheet of sandpaper grit-side-up on a sheet of plywood, and then rub the sawn edges down to a smooth, straight finish.

the line of cut a little to the waste side of the drawn line (FIG. 14-5). At this stage, don't cut out any of the slots and notches; just settle for fretting out the three identical outside-edge profiles. *Note:* It is most important that the cut is at right angles to the surface.

8. Number the three components 1, 2, and 3. Number 1 is the complete shape with the pierced slot. Number 2 is the basic shape but with the ⅜-inch-wide entrance slot. Number 3 is the most complicated, with a ½-inch-wide entrance

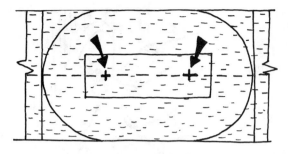

14-4 Draw in the centerline, strike off the ½-inch-wide central slot, set the compass to a radius of ¾ inch, and draw out the half-circle end-curves. The arrows show the position of the compass point.

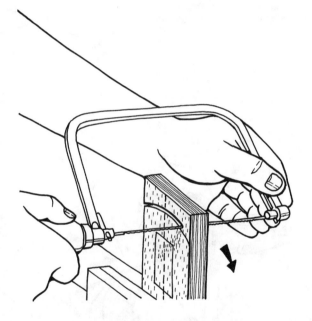

14-5 Keep changing both the position of the wood in the vice and the angle of approach, so that the coping saw is always presented with the line of best cut.

slot and a ½-inch-wide, ⅛-inch-deep inside notch. See the design template (FIG. 14-1).

9. Take component number 1—the one with the central slot—set the ³⁄₁₆-inch bit in the drill, and run a saw blade pilot hole through the central area of waste (FIG. 14-6). This done, secure the component in the vice, take the coping saw and unhitch the blade, pass the blade through the pilot hole (FIG. 14-7), refit and retension the blade, and carefully cut out the bulk of waste. Cut about ¹⁄₁₆ inch to the waste side of the drawn line.

10. When you come to cutting out the waste from components 2 and 3, repeat the cutting procedure with the coping saw—only this time of course—you

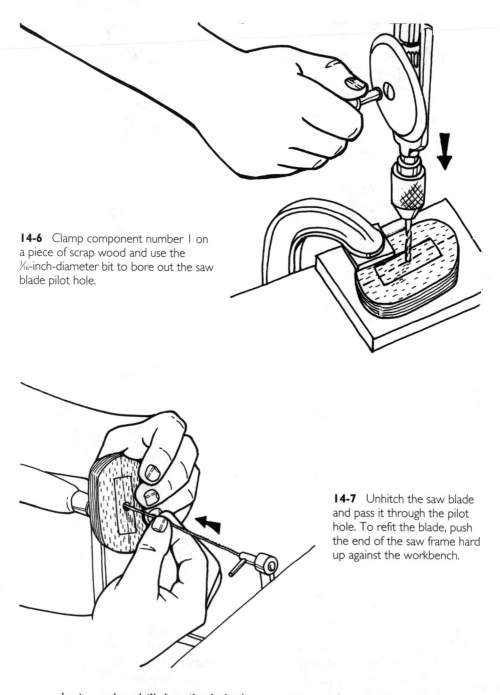

14-6 Clamp component number 1 on a piece of scrap wood and use the ³⁄₁₆-inch-diameter bit to bore out the saw blade pilot hole.

14-7 Unhitch the saw blade and pass it through the pilot hole. To refit the blade, push the end of the saw frame hard up against the workbench.

don't need to drill the pilot hole, but can cut straight into the waste from the edge of the profile.

11. Having cleared away the bulk of the waste to within about ¹⁄₁₆ inch of the drawn line, set the components flat-down on a slab of scrap wood, and use

the bevel-edged chisel to carefully slice cut back all the sawn edges to the drawn lines. The chisel must be razor sharp (FIG. 14-8).

12. Be watchful, when you are cutting back true to the marked lines, that the primary ½-×-1½-inch slot doesn't become sloppy and grow in size. If all is correct, you should be able to push any component end-on through the central slot of any other component. The best procedure is to slice away at the edges—a little by little—all the while stopping to check for fit.

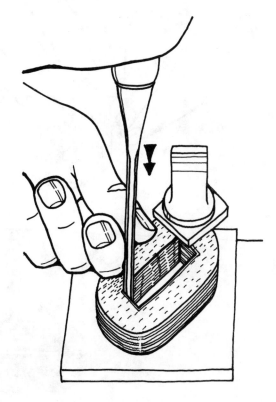

14-8 Clamp the puzzle piece on some scrap wood and use the bevel-edged chisel to very carefully slice and pare the sawn edges back to the drawn line.

13. When you have achieved a good tight push-fit with all three components, take the fine-graded sandpaper—stuck grit-side-up to a board and a stick—and rub all faces and edges down to crisp, smooth, square finish (FIG. 14-9).

14. Wipe away all the dust and give all surfaces a couple of coats of black spirit pen ink. Lay on one coat, let it soak in, and then lay on another coat.

15. When the spirit ink stain is completely dry, give the whole puzzle—all three components—a generous coat of furniture wax and burnish them to a dull-sheen finish.

16. And now to put the puzzle together . . . !

   • Take component number 1 and slide it up and over component number 2 so that the entrance slot is just about clear (FIG. 14-10, top).

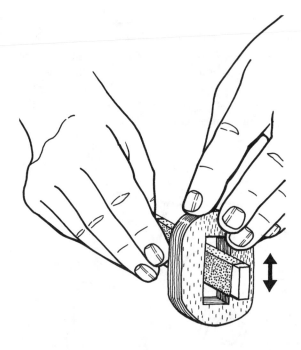

14-9 Rub the edges down to a perfectly true and square finish.

14-10 (top) Slide component number 2 through component number 1 so that the slot is left clear. (bottom) Hold component number 3 so that the slot is facing downwards, and then slide it over components 1 and 2.

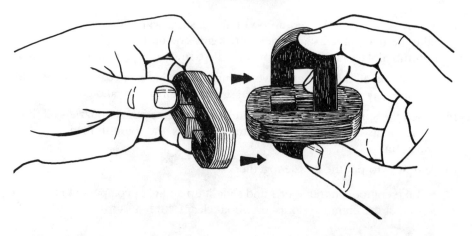

- Take component number 3, hold it so that the entrance slot is downwards, and slide it over the end of number 1 and towards the center of number 2 (FIG. 14-10, bottom).
- Push number 3 into the center of the slot and let number 2 drop down to lock the puzzle. Easy, ain't it? Ha!

WATCHPOINTS

If you like the idea of the project, but are not so keen about using the coping saw, you could speed up the working stages by using a scroll saw. Work well within the waste wood margin, and cut back with the chisel to the design lines.

The wood needs to be completely dry. If you start by using slightly damp wood, the components pieces will dry out and shrink, and you will be left with a loose-fitting puzzle.

If you don't much like the idea of using plywood, then you could use a dense close-grained hardwood like beech.

If you decide to color the component pieces with paint, be careful that the buildup of paint or varnish doesn't change the sizes to the extent that the puzzle pieces wedge and get stuck.

Spirit felt-tip pens can stain hands, clothes, and worksurfaces. It's best to wear gloves and work on scrap paper.

Index

caution points, 151
grid drawing, 145
sanding instructions, 146
tools and materials, 143
vise and drilling diagram, 150
woods, 143

K

king's castellated castle, 10-23
  caregivers' guide, 12
  caution points, 23
  gluing diagrams, 19
  grid drawing, 13
  painting diagram, 20-22
  template design, 14
  tools and materials, 11
  vise and cutting diagram, 15, 16, 17
  vise and drilling diagram, 18
  woods, 11

M

monkey memo, 24-35
  bevel diagram, 30
  caregivers' guide, 26
  caution points, 35
  chiseling diagram, 31-32
  fretsaw diagram, 32
  grid drawing, 27
  scoring the wood diagram, 29
  template design, 27
  tools and materials, 25
  woods, 25

P

puzzle cross, 152-161
  assembly, diagram, 160
  caregivers' guide, 153-154
  caution points, 161
  compass work, 157
  coping saw diagram, 157
  grid drawing, 155
  tools and materials, 153
  vise and drilling diagram, 158
  woods, 153

S

shelf, 97-106
  caregivers' guide, 98-99
  caution points, 106
  compass work, 102
  drilling and sawing diagram, 103
  grid drawing, 100

template design, 101
tools and materials, 98
woods, 98
sled, 107-118
  assembly diagram, 117
  caregivers' guide, 109
  caution points, 118
  cutting diagram, 112, 114-115
  grid drawing, 110
  template design, 111
  tools and materials, 108
  vise and drilling diagram, 116
  woods, 108
stilts, 47-59
  caregivers' guide, 49
  caution points, 59
  coping saw diagram, 54
  grid drawing, 50
  measurement diagram, 56
  painting diagram, 57, 58
  template design, 51
  tools and materials, 48
  vise and drilling diagram, 52
  woods, 48

T

tools and materials,
  airplane, 73
  bathtub yacht, 2
  door knocker, 61
  drafting table, 120
  duck targets, 84
  eagle emblem, 131
  jewelry, 143
  king's castellated castle, 11
  monkey memo, 25
  puzzle cross, 153
  sled, 108
  stilts, 48
  shelf, 98
  whirler, 37

W

whirler, 36-46
  caregivers' guide, 38
  caution points, 46
  chiseling diagram, 45
  cutting the wood, 40-41
  grid drawing, 39
  tools and materials, 37
  vise and drilling diagram, 43-44
  woods, 37